Life/Work Coaching

and the process of

SELF DISCOVERY

"A Guide for Emotional Healing"

Life/Work Coaching

and the process of

SELF DISCOVERY

~~~~~~~~~~~~~

A Guide for Emotional Healing

Linda Parsons

... with John Selby
~~~~~~~~~~~~~

Front & back cover design by Aisling Conneely

Printed in the United States of America

ISBN-13: 978-1-962984-16-4 print edition
ISBN-13: 978-1-962984-17-1 e-book edition

Published by Waterside Productions
2055 Oxford Ave, Cardiff, CA 92007
www.waterside.com

Dedication

To My Brother Frederick

1969 - 2023

If one advances confidently in the
Direction of his dreams, & endeavors
To live the life he has imagined, he will
Meet with a success unexpected in common hours.

Henry David Thoreau

Table of Contents

~~~~~~~~~~~~~~~~~~~~~~~~~~~~
~~~~~~~~~~~~~~~~~~~~~~~~~~~~

Prologue

by John Selby

~~~~~~~~~~~~~~~~~~~~~~

Linda and I came together by what is often called pure chance. She was rereading one of my books, *Tapping The Source*, and also working with my *Let Love Find You* process, and went online to check out my website – and just spontaneously emailed my contact address ... and pow! That initial connection quite rapidly expanded into my taking a look at her rough manuscript of *Self Discovery*.

Even though we live 5,000 miles apart, at deeper levels we discovered that we're highly congruent. We've both spent most of our lives focused on how to help clients heal emotionally and grow into a fulfilling life. And we've both been inspired to try and write meaningful and impactful books to share what we've discovered. So right away I took special interest in what she had to offer in her book.

During my first reading of her manuscript I realized that she'd produced a diamond in the rough. She's been out in the field actually working day in and day out with people suffering, often quite seriously, so she speaks directly from her own challenges and victories. She guides her clients confidently toward the healing light of emotional recovery and spiritual adventure. Even when dealing with intense topics, her tone remains hopeful, encouraging, and trustworthy. Her voice is loud and clear, and yet also gentle and compassionate.

I helped her with the polish edits of *Self Discovery* and in the process, after all my years of inner exploration, found myself expanding yet another notch on my personal journey. So I can
~~~~~~~~~~~~~~~~~~~~~~

highly recommend this book for all of us, no matter where we are in our unique life adventure.

For people just now beginning to explore ways to accelerate their inner growth and healing, the experience of reading this book and practicing the exercises and meditations will stimulate insight, hope, and healing. And as I mentioned, for those of us further along the self-discovery trail, this book can wake up new realizations into who we really are, and shine light on inner dimensions still awaiting our exploration.

For me, and Linda equally, the amazing thing about being alive as humans on this planet is that we're seemingly infinite in our capacity to expand our personal awareness as we become more and more conscious of the vastness of creation. Linda's book helps us choose to dedicate our lives to fulfilling our unique participation in this multi-dimensional vastness.

Self Discovery is a highly pragmatic book because throughout, Linda is focused on what she knows actually works. Each of the ten chapters in this book explores a core aspect of life coaching and therapy work, in language everyone can readily grasp. I love this pragmatic tone! Whether this is mostly new to you or a valued refresher course, enjoy every page – and also take time to explore the short exercises and meditations you'll encounter along the way.

John Selby

New Years Day 2024
Santa Cruz, California

INTRODUCTION

~~~~~~~~~~~~~~~~~~~~~~~~

Life is a mirror and will
reflect back to the thinker
what he thinks into it.

Ernest Holmes

The information and insights offered in this book are designed to provide you with helpful guidance, and also shed light on how a life coach works to support your inner growth, healing and fulfillment. The following chapters are filled with tips and insights from my therapist/life coach's toolkit. Take whatever resonates with you, and apply it to your life.

I've always been curious about what makes us tick. I've studied and worked with many therapy techniques, systems and strategies – what I'm sharing with you here is what works for me and my clients. The popular concept of coaching of course originated in the sport world. Applied to any profession or life situation, coaching aims to unlock people's potential to maximize their performance and sense of personal fulfillment.

Coaching helps people learn for themselves. We all have a built-in natural self-learning and self-discovery capability that is actually disrupted by a teacher's 'do this and now this' instruction. We're like acorns, each of which contains within it all the potential to be a magnificent oak tree. Yes, we often need nourishment, encouragement, and the vision to reach upward toward the light of fulfillment – but our oak-tree-ness
~~~~~~~~~~~~~~~~~~~~~~~~

is already within us. The job of the coach is to ensure that their clients are moving with confidence and clarity toward inner balance and engaged success.

As a coach I am continually practicing what's called empathic listening – taking in both what's being said and also what's not being said. Listening to a client's emotional tone of voice, and watching their body language, enables me to perceive their deeper thoughts, feelings and realizations, and then feed all this back to them. I use my own intuition to spot what's missing from the conversation, and encourage new insights to naturally emerge during a session.

My initial role is to ask questions and make observations that help unlock a buried issue, or cast new light on a bothersome situation. As a coach, I win when my client wins. Rather than trying to stuff someone into any preconceived role or goal, I aim to help clients discover for themselves their deeper aspirations – and then I explore with them the optimal path to achieving their goals. My pleasure comes from being part of someone's personal process as I help them identify and carry forth with strategies that lead toward desired results.

In life coaching, the subtle process of nurturing emotional intelligence is very important – and the key to attaining a high level of emotional intelligence is deepening our relationship with ourselves. This is achieved through enhancing and focusing our core moment-to-moment inner awareness. After all, without awareness we're simply not present. This is why heightened mindfulness is so important – it directly awakens the self-discovery process. And then self-inquiry enables my clients to be better equipped to relate more deeply and honestly with everyone they encounter.

In coaching I rely strongly on my intuition to guide me during a coaching conversation. I'm continually learning to become more receptive to this subtle form of realization and communication. Said another way, I strive to move beyond intellectual analysis so I can tap directly into heart-centered insights and suggestions. I also do my best to include a good sense of humor in the process – because when used appropriately, humor helps encourage relaxation, opening up a lightness that allows space for inner discoveries and spontaneous insights.

Listening and relating intuitively rather than analytically is an art that evolves and unfolds throughout our lives. Overall I think this process of mindful listening is misunderstood and underrated as a crucial life skill. As a coach I strive to listen ever more closely and effectively, and teach my clients to listen to themselves in this expanded mode.

Highly-receptive listening is key to what makes life coaching uniquely effective. When coach and client are listening to each other with enhanced sensitivity and mutual acceptance and trust, unexpected insights into healing and fulfillment can readily emerge.

A parallel aspect to listening deeply to each other is learning how to listen with full nonjudgmental attention to our own deeper inner voice. As we'll explore in depth later on, we mostly listen to the pushing chatterbox ego voice inside our heads. But too often our ego voice is fear-fixated, detached from our deeper voice of wisdom – and it's often downright neurotic and self-delusional. Learning to quiet the ego voice and instead tune into our heart-centered voice of intuition and spiritual guidance is therefore a primary goal in any mindful life-coaching relationship.

I love this definition of a life coach:

I am here to hold space for you,
to ask powerful direct questions,

to help you uncover and dissolve
your limiting beliefs –
to help you move through any fear
or worry that is keeping you from your best life.

I'm not here to give you advice
or to fix anything for you.
Using a variety of tools and techniques,
I'll help you reconnect with your inner wisdom
so you can guide yourself to your right life.

Once connected to your own guidance system,
I'll walk alongside you as you dream
and scheme about a life that will
bring you more joy.

And from there, we'll work together
to create 'turtle steps' to bring
your dreams into reality.

Suzanne Trainor

Nothing New Under The Sun

A life coach aims to help people break free from chronic blockages in their inherent creativity and awareness. The underlying theory and logic of such self-discovery has been emerging in our world culture for countless generations. Spiritual and philosophical teachers such as Buddha and Jesus and so forth from many different historic traditions have been telling us how best to live our lives. But it seems that far too few of our ancestors were actually listening – thus the ongoing need for the deeper truths and methodologies to be said anew.

With this in mind, we're continually updating ancient wisdom into our current cultural mindset. What has been revealed and taught long before needs to be expressed again in our just-appearing scientific, psychological and spiritual framework. And we're also now rapidly evolving and advancing our understanding of how the brain works, how attitudes, beliefs, intentions and emotions influence each other, and how our quality of consciousness determines the outcome of our lives.

New clients initially say to me, "Well I already know all about that, I read about it in a book." But I remind them that learning something secondhand as a concept is not enough. To gain true creative power, knowledge must become active and applied. We must shift from being passive thinkers to being active experiencers. Impactful knowledge and creativity come from actually experiencing something with our senses and with our hearts. And once we know something directly in this manner, once we feed our minds with true experiences of the outside world and our inner feelings, then our minds and bodies can become expressions of this knowledge – and we become valued creators.

In sum: life coaches aren't just busy teaching clients theoretically about life. We're helping clients learn to discover, envision and create the life they deep-down desire. The human mind is by nature creative, which means realistically that we can act to create the life we want. I'm sure you know that your mind is your most powerful asset. It's not an exaggeration to say that your mind is the greatest gift you've been given by the infinite creative source. As we'll be exploring throughout this book, your mind is all you have. Remove the mind and ... lights out. Focus your attention in valued directions and ... lights on!

You are a creative being creating moment-to-moment the world you seek. My role as a coach is to help you in that creative act – not imposing my mold on your life, but helping you discover your own unique path. Being creative doesn't mean you must become a painter, sculptor, writer or poet. Each of us can be creative in any endeavor and walk of life. It makes no difference what particular expression your creativity assumes – what matters is being open to explore and manifest whatever wants to be expressed through you.

Maybe you're exploring something that thousands or millions of people have already done before you. What's important is your unique expression of that truth or beauty or realization out into your present-moment world. And as the saying goes: be sure you don't die with your song still hidden inside you. Not everyone can be a great singer or leader or inventor, but everyone can be uniquely expressive. And as we often discover in coaching, becoming more creative is also a natural healing process.

Becoming more expressive, spontaneous and responsive is at the deepest levels also a great way to stay in tune with existence itself. When you open up and begin to express your true self in whatever form you choose, the infinite realms of consciousness will become empowered to manifest newness through you. And luckily, creating is a skill you can learn like any other skill, as you develop mastery over time.

Unfortunately most people have not been taught how to be creators – so we must now learn for ourselves how to be the creative agent in our own lives. It's not just another overused cliché – we do create our own reality. And that's in essence what can be learned when working with a life coach.

A lot of people create their lives unconsciously by default rather than by design. They allow their inherited or adopted life circumstances to dictate what happens to them – and so usually they remain dissatisfied and subject to the whims of their situation. Entire lives can pass by like that – dealing chronically with one life complication after another. Then when we're seventy or eighty years old we realize we never really created the life we deep-down wanted, the life of our personal choosing.

The role of a life coach is to point their clients toward an entirely different way to approach life. This can feel like a quantum shift – accepting the challenge to become a proactive agent in the present moment. Why not live your life as a grounded and inspired initiator who envisions what your deeper self hungers for – and then actively creates that life?

Our Creative Origins

We were all naturally expressive and creative as children. When a baby is ready to start walking, it feels spontaneously in tune with its innate nature. Its body and mind know how to learn to walk, to talk, to move out and be fully present and creative in the world. It will endure a lot of bumps and falls but it doesn't give up – it keeps going until finally the day comes when it takes a few steps on its own.

Now as an adult you can choose to let go of social inhibitions and negative attitudes, and reconnect with the spontaneous positive being that you really are. Humans are the only creatures in the known universe who have been given a tool to create with – our amazing minds connected with our loving hearts. Within reason, we can manifest whatever we decide to create. And yet too often we seem to go out of our way not to use our creative powers.

Our mind is what shapes our decisions, habits, character and ultimately our destiny. Sow a thought ... reap a deed. Sow a deed ... reap a habit. Sow a habit ... reap a character. Sow a character ... reap a destiny. A life coach provides the seed, the idea, the possibility. Together, coach and client work to nurture that seed toward its ultimate life fulfillment.

I hope you enjoy this productive journey into self-discovery.

CHAPTER ONE

Beyond The Neurotic Ego

~~~~~~~~~~~~~~~~~~~~~~~~~~~~

A human being is part of the whole –
a part limited in time and space.
And yet we experience ourselves,
our thoughts and feelings,
as something separated from the rest.

Albert Einstein

We all know first-hand that we have a dominant 'executive' function of our brain associated with the frontal lobe and pre-frontal cortex. This uniquely-human part of our brain enables us to think rationally or irrationally, judge constantly, plan ahead, reflect on memories, worry about the future – and actively direct our every moment. The word *ego*, which comes from Greek and Latin roots, originally meant "I am" or simply "I".

The term has been used in many quote-differing ways over the last hundred years since Freud made the term popular in his psychotherapy writings. For most people, the ego is the ever-present strong mental force that drives us. A healthy ego is a marvelous thing – It knows when to step forward and push us into action, and it also knows when to step back and surrender control to our deeper intuitions, feelings and aspirations. The ego when not neurotic can evaluate a situation and determine what's best to do next. It can dominate the mind with its inner monologue, but it can also drop into silence when appropriate,
~~~~~~~~~~~~~~~~~~~~~~~~~~~~

so that we can hear and respond to our more-intuitive voice of wisdom and guidance.

If we were blessed with parents who themselves had a healthy, balanced, integrated ego presence, from the womb onward we began to develop our own healthy 'executive function'. We learned how to observe reality just as it is, to respond accordingly, and do what must be done to gain and maintain a satisfactory flow in our lives. When the ego is healthy and not neurotic, we don't need a life coach – we're doing fine on our own.

The problem arises when the natural ego function of the mind becomes neurotic – when we become chronically caught up in excessive and often-irrational anxiety, stress and depression. Ego-neurosis develops when that mental function becomes caught up in delusions about reality, and fixates on the negative – feeling inadequate, unloved, in danger, afraid, confused, out of touch with our deeper sense of intuitive guidance and wellbeing.

Almost always a neurotic defensive ego develops early in life, in the first six years. If we're born into an anxious judgmental family, we're probably going to become anxious ourselves. Recent research documents that even in the womb an infant will be strongly impacted by the emotional resonance of the mother. And in early childhood a toddler will unavoidably feel emotions it picks up from its caregivers.

I'm talking about this basic human dynamic because it's much of what a coach will need to focus on if there's to be significant and lasting improvement in the client's sense of self. Basically if in childhood our ego developed in a neurotic constricted fearful way, as adults we will need to deal with this head-on. And because the very nature of a neurotic ego is to totally take over a person's sense of self, often some outside coaching guidance is needed in order to help the client break free from ego dominance.

I'm not Freudian and I'm using the term ego in a different way. Over the years I've explored various coaching and therapy approaches, and hopefully this book offers an integration of coaching techniques into a holistic approach.

We all at times feel desperation, depression, shame, guilt, low self-esteem and all the rest of the negative human emotions. This is natural, and accepting and even embracing the full spectrum of human emotions is the wise path, rather than rejecting the negatives. The ego voice will try to dominate – but with dedication and practice, we can learn to heal our early emotional wounds, develop a healthy ego, and get on with our lives.

Neurotic anxiety and chronic judgment can grip not only just an individual but also an entire culture. Just watch the evening news – our entire world civilization is living in constant stressful apprehensions and antagonisms. There's the horrendous worldwide fear of nuclear war, climate disaster, micro-plastic contamination, regional food shortages, violent extremist threats and so forth. We're held by the media in a state of chronic anxiety and depression.

But this is not being caused just by 'things out there'. Each of us embodies this anxiety state. Our own minds continually generate and broadcast thoughts and imaginations, attitudes and emotions that perpetuate our shared neurotic fears. The fear-based ego function of the mind dominates our collective experience. The inherent power of fear unfortunately overrides the more positive qualities of the human spirit – and this keeps us from expressing or even realizing our deeper authentic selves.

Related to this, as a coach I do have some very strong beliefs and understandings about this dilemma, and our way beyond the dilemma. For instance, the truth as I see it is that we're all born with an authentic sense of who we really are as unique participants in a greater universal whole. We can refer to our inherent human sense of authentic identity in scientific, psychological, philosophical or spiritual terms – the words all aim toward a very real aspect of our lives. We speak of wisdom, intuitive insight, religious guidance and personal integrity. And we speak of 'falling from grace' and developing a false sense of self, a phony ego personality that overrides our true nature and personality.

The responsibility of coaching for me is dominated by the challenge of helping a client observe their ingrained neurotic or obsessive thoughts and behaviors that are ego-driven – and step by step learn effective ways to calm and quiet that anxious ego. However, I don't see this as a battle. I see it as the opportunity to tune regularly into other dimensions of consciousness, as we reeducate our ego into a more realistic and heart-centered sense of self.

The Ego's Illusion Of Separation

The ego's goal is, quite explicitly, ego autonomy.
From the beginning its purpose is to be
separate, sufficient unto itself and
independent of any power except its own.

A Course In Miracles

So – who are we really? In childhood we inevitably developed a unique sense of our own identity. We were born with a bright spirit, an authentic self. But we had to also develop a social self, a personality mask that was acceptable to our parents, our community, our society. We had to repress doing things that brought punishment, and try to put on an often-false front and even phony mask. So much of what we had to do in order to fit into our family, community, educational and business world constantly pushed us into identifying with our social identity, and in the process we repressed our deeper sense of who we are.

And this is where the ego function of the mind came to dominate our identity. This is of course a vastly complex process, but it's one we all went through. We lost touch with our own authentic feelings and wisdom – and now we need to reclaim that authentic self. Why? Because a fearful ego is not at all fun to be around. A dominant dictatorial ego, like any heartless tyrant, will not serve our higher good.

Key point: A neurotic ego almost always insists that it's all there is to you. This is illusory, and that's just what neurosis is all about – distorting reality. A neurotic ego also demands that your sense of individual selfhood is seen as entirely separate and isolated from everything 'out there'. It's you against the universe. And – as long as it holds you in its anxious grip, your ego self will maintain this illusion until you call its bluff.

Once 'the greater you' decides to break free, to expand beyond the ego's anxious domination, once you learn to focus on other dimensions of who you are beyond your fear-based false front, the ego begins to lose its dominance over your thoughts and moods. As you remove the power of your attention from the ego's illusions, they in fact begin to fade and ... be gone.

Notice each morning when you wake up, how your ego mind instantly fixates on half a dozen lurking scenarios you need to deal with that day. Rather than enjoying the present moment and focusing on thankfulness just for being alive, you probably tend to run through your entire day in future-fixated worry/stress mode (anxiety) or past-fixated self-judgment and guilt/shame mode (depression). What we're focusing on in this book is your inner freedom and power to determine where you focus your attention moment to moment. You do have the power to choose – once you realize it.

The result of being locked into chronic negative mental fixations is that your deeper, wiser, happier and more hopeful authentic self hardly ever gets a chance to shine – to speak to you with positive ideas and begin to influence what happens in your emerging life. Because our ego feels responsible for us, and is too often consumed in anxiety and depression, our lives tend to lack lightness, clarity, harmony and all the other positive human feelings and insights. Chronic worry overrides other more-positive functions of the mind.

Because most of us are caught up daily in this habitual anxious state, we tend to assume this fear-gripped habit of the ego mind is our natural human condition. I myself have struggled with this negative state of worry and pain, and devoted much of my life to finding the best ways to transcend my worried ego and regain connection with my natural non-anxious spirit. What you'll find in this book are the most effective approaches that do seem to transcend a non-stop worried mind.

I want to repeat that maintaining a healthy ego is essential to survival. It plays an uplifting pragmatic role in what we want to do with our lives. When our ego function is working confidently to understand, plan and act upon our deeper heart-felt intentions, our lives are good! Only when linked to fear-based emotions and imaginations do our ego-thoughts become neurotic and reactionary.

The next time you take a shower, just quietly monitor all the various thoughts that arise spontaneously during that shower. Are you peacefully enjoying the shower experience – or are you habitually, almost compulsively having one anxious thought after another pop into your mind, about people and situations, memories and future apprehensions that provoke negative emotions – and in turn more anxious thoughts?

Here's a key thing about the ego – it is almost exclusively fixated on the past and the future. When you're relaxing into a hot shower in the sensory present moment, notice that your worried thoughts are temporarily silent. Right then is when positive intuitive thoughts have a chance to speak to you. I have found that it's almost impossible to force your chatterbox ego voice to shut up. But what you can do is learn ways to shift your focus of attention away from worry mode, toward more rewarding thoughts and feelings.

What does the ego mind really fear? Why does it get so uptight and defensive? Well in the first years of life, toddlers don't have the mental capacity to think about the past or to imagine what might happen in the future. They live spontaneously in the moment – and when free from their parental worries and judgments, they naturally play and explore and enjoy the present moment – and adults love to be around that positive brightness of youthful spirit toddlers exude.

Untraumatized young children feel that they're a natural organic part of the greater whole – they feel they belong, they're safe, they're accepted and valued and loved just as they are. But then as they become more aware, and learn to talk and evaluate and think, something not so good happens. They get scolded and punished when they do certain things – they feel judged and threatened and begin to lose their sense of belonging. And this paves the way for the ego to try to take over.

I repeat – the ego is not essentially bad, not at all. Its evolutionary purpose is to protect a child's physical and emotional wellbeing. And it will do everything it can to avoid pain and judgment. When the parents have healthy balanced egos, their child will probably not develop a dominating neurotic ego. But in reality, most parents are themselves struggling with their own fear-based attitudes, assumptions and reactions. So it's good to realize that we're all caught up in this together. No one is to blame – and everyone is responsible.

When the ego function of the brain begins to kick into gear, a child begins to realize that it is in fact a separate biological entity, that it has a quite distinct mind and body – and that if it doesn't learn to control itself and behave it'll run into trouble, experience pain, and in extreme situations perhaps get excluded from its family and community.

We all went through this ego-birth step. It's often referred to as the socialization process. We simply must learn to control ourselves – otherwise pain and fear will ensue. This fear of rejection and expulsion is a core biological programming – and the ego emerges to protect the child from abandonment and ultimately a terrible solitary death. So out of fear the ego is born. We must develop a cognitive function that makes sure we don't get cast out of our community.

Therefore the development of an ego-controller is a universal childhood process. We are indeed separate, and yet we must be part of our community or we'll perhaps perish. And out of this fear the ego emerges – and unfortunately the ego function tends to take over a child's mind. Almost every moment becomes fixated on thoughts and actions trying to avoid or escape something bad happening in the future. And yet deep-down we all know that there's a free spirit inside us, a bright intuitive loving personality that hungers to break free and express itself.

For me, coaching involves nurturing the development of a harmonious relationship between a healthy ego and our free inner spirit. Even if we've developed a seriously-dominating ego, we still have the power to strengthen deeper aspects of our self. We can learn to overcome our constrictive feelings of separation and isolation, and regain our sense of belonging, of being an integral part of the greater whole. This inner healing process might take time to accomplish – but the rewards are definitely worth it.

Here's a beginning insight into this inner transformation: over the years your ego has developed a worldview all its own. And this often-distorted view is grounded on the belief that you are completely on your own in life, it's you versus the outside world – and therefore you must continually be on guard and struggle to defend and advance yourself, to become somebody of importance, to fight and attain individual recognition, financial security, relationship dominance and other anxiety-based victories.

Now let's contrast this fear-based ego-stance with the deeper truth of life, as both spiritual teachers and scientific experts regularly state – that we are not separate, even though our ego insists we are. Perhaps the most important commandments Jesus and Buddha both focused on are the following words: "Fear not"... and "Love one another." These words seem aimed directly to the human ego. Spiritual teachings have continually brought these life-themes to the fore – and yet look at how dominant the self-centered fear-based ego still is. After two thousand years we're still stuck in ego-dominance mode, constantly locked into battling against a hostile ever-threatening world rather than focusing on how we can work together for the wellbeing of all.

For me, here's the resolution to this universal dilemma – and it's been around for thousands of years. Our primary power is our ability to determine, moment to moment, where we're going to focus our mind's power of attention. As the ancient Hawaiian tradition says, "Energy flows where attention goes." Where we focus our attention determines what we will manifest. If we keep on focusing in anxious defensive directions, we're going to remain stuck in that fearful mode. But we can choose to focus our attention elsewhere. We can stop giving attention and energy to anxious and depressed thoughts, feelings and situations – and instead nurture what brings us joy, clarity, insight and fulfillment.

Definitely the greatest challenge we face in today's society is learning to actively allocate our most valuable resource in positive creative directions. Shall we choose to keep paying attention to our fearful egotistic voice, or to our voice of inspiration, the voice of Spirit? Just realizing we have this choice can be a landmark in our evolving lives.

Many Voices To Choose From

All of us find ourselves listening to various voices talking to us in our heads, and we also go around imagining what we want to say to various people – forever rehearsing defensive stances we'll probably never take in reality. We even carry on mental conversations with people who are already dead and gone. And the sad thing is, we don't seem to ever resolve these conflicts.

Freud coined the term 'super-ego' to identify our internal voice that's chronically accusing us of doing something wrong, or criticizing us for something we failed to do. So many parents talk judgmentally at their children. Again, it's not their fault – they most likely had their own parents doing the same to them. But the result is the often-permanent installation of a judgmental inner voice of authority that's constantly knocking down the child, and also the adult who still hears that nagging mean negative voice.

And what does the child do in reaction as a defense? Almost universally that child will develop the habit of defending itself to the parent, trying to justify its behavior, struggling to prove its own self-worth. The result is a never-ending conflict that can consume a person's inner life.

So. Already we have twin voices in our heads – the voice of the condemning parent or teacher, and the defensive child's voice struggling to gain the parent's understanding and approval. If you start watching the voices in your head, you'll almost surely discover both of these. There's definitely a still-youthful 'you' who's talking to that judgmental, basically imaginary voice in your head – the internalized voice of authority, your super-ego.

Often you won't even remember the particular scene where you were shouted at or humiliated or shamed by that voice in reality – but you compulsively keep arguing with that voice. The trouble is, you never seem to win. The next time you're in the shower or commuting or whatever, you'll find yourself again putting up defensive arguments showing that hey, you're okay, you're not guilty, you're not worthless!

Again, focus closely on who those condemning put-down voices actually were in your youthful history – the voices of your parents and other people who had power over you, who shouted at you, threatened you and disciplined you. They condemned your behavior and gave orders for you to control yourself and do what your elders told you to do – or else. And these same voices quite early became the foundation of your budding ego.

This all happens fairly unconsciously and unnoticed. At some point a dominant adult voice takes over and speaks to the child as an internalized authority in charge of the child's whole life. With a budding ego, this of course can serve the positive purpose of helping the child learn to be good and fit into society. Those voices can be kind and loving as well as harsh and threatening. But when they insist they represent the real and only you, when they distort reality and become constantly judgmental rather than nurturing, then problems inevitably develop.

This inner critic is the greatest fault-finder. It continually seeks out memories and perceived personality faults that it judges as embarrassing, shameful, sinful, dumb, weak, bad and so forth. And as most therapists and life coaches know first-hand, these internalized self-induced judgments can leave a young person emotionally devastated. They contribute to feelings of confusion, anger, depression and low self-esteem. And again – the inner critic usually sounds very much like an internalized judgmental father-figure, a demanding mother, priest or teacher who has somehow taken up residence in the child's mind.

I don't mean to put down all the parents and teachers who think they're helping a child succeed in life by judging and criticizing their youthful attitudes and behavior. Traditionally parents and teachers have assumed that it's their job to point out where a child is messing up. But in trying to be of help, they too often damage rather than help a child. Still charged with their own internalized critic, they're broadcasting fear and aggression, dominance and rejection that continue to pollute their supposedly-helpful judgments and attacks. They continue to pass on to the next generation the damaging abuse they themselves experienced in their own childhood.

As we'll see later on, one of the vital steps in breaking free from your own inner critic will be to finally forgive the adults whose voices have infected your own mind. Somehow the multi-generational continuation of this universal human pattern must be stopped – and using the power of forgiveness to end inner-critic suffering is one of the best ways to get this job done.

When you look inward, you can note for yourself that a neurotic ego is always demanding, it's a dictator insisting on managing and limiting a child's entire sense of self. This might be okay if the ego-voice is wise, compassionate, intuitive and playful. But like all dictators, the neurotic ego is none of those. That voice that's so dominant is devious, secretive – and always insisting that there is no self beyond its phony defensive false front.

And so perhaps you became a helpless victim, you lost your broader sense of identity beyond the ego – end of story. But wait – like I said earlier, there is also a brighter you in retreat but still alive and begging to emerge. You probably still have many moments when your ego voice dies down and suddenly you feel relieved, you feel a taste of upsurging joy in your heart, and you suddenly rediscover a quite-different voice and presence way down deeper in your heart – a voice that wants to sing, to burst forth and finally experience liberation!

Who are you when you learn to let go of regrets from your past and worries about the future, and instead focus your attention upon the eternal present moment? And how can you achieve this liberation? Well for a starter, that's what meditation is all about at its core. When you regularly take time to tune into your breathing and your bodily sensations, and enjoy the pure inflowing experience of simply being alive here and now, you move into position to rediscover who you really are.

When you stop listening to your inner critic and instead start listening for inputs from your deeper inner voice – guess what? You discover that there is indeed a mysterious intuitive realm where you can receive heart-centered rather than head-centered guidance.

When you take your next shower, first of all notice if there's currently a negative flow of dialog that goes on in your mind between you and your inner critic. And then notice what happens when you choose to focus purely upon the present moment, on feeling good in your body, on breathing into newness – and see if without any provocation or pushing, you tap into something beyond your ego ... but something definitely you.

Often this guidance isn't an actual inner vocal communication with words and memories and so forth – often it's a sudden effortless flash of a deep insight or realization. When you feel separate and isolated, contracted with worries and confusion and depression, this positive inner voice of wisdom and guidance cannot be tapped into. But as soon as you learn to transcend the ego, you open yourself to all the rest of you. You find your authentic voice at last, you feel grounded in your heart and in the universe – you are free to express your authentic self beyond your ego-programmed identity.

Authentic Truth

Jesus is quoted as saying, "Know the Truth, and the Truth will set you free." This is an ultimate guideline for life, The Truth lives within us, it's not just an academic concept we can learn in school. And the ego is not known for being unbiased, for having deep wisdom, for being connected with and influenced by anything deeper than itself. Rather, we know Truth when we actually feel it resonating in our hearts, in our souls.

It's of course important to develop a sense of authentic truth in our lives. We all know it's not socially accepted to go around hearing voices in our heads. Culturally we're all afraid of being judged as crazy, and crazy people hear voices in their heads – so let's avoid that at all cost, right? No, mostly wrong. Only one percent of the population is schizophrenic, driven crazy by inner voices. What we're talking about here is something quite different, and the experience almost universal.

We've seen that there are multiple voices inside our heads. Does this mean that we have multiple personalities? In fact, in a way, yes. It's a cultural myth to assume that each of us has just one fixed personality all the time. Who we are is always situational. You know that you assume a different tone and presence when you talk with different people. Your personality shifts if you go from talking to your mom to talking to a policeman or a friend or lover. In fact you are whoever you become in the current situation you're engaged in. Yes, you have your life story, but is this story non-changing? As we'll see you can evolve your narrative about your past and who you truly are, as you deepen your evolving sense of your authentic self.

Notice who you are in the shower when you catch yourself arguing internally with your super-ego. What tone of voice, what mood, what stance do you speak from when defending your self-worth from your inner critic? Is this the same you who talks pillow talk with your lover or goofs off with a young child?

I might mention here that there's a whole line of therapy that's quite effective, called positive self-talk counseling. So many of us go around talking negatively to our own selves, totally internalizing the super-ego, telling ourselves we can't do something, that we're not ready or capable, that we're ugly or dumb or hopeless. This internal put-down habit is so common – but we can learn to talk right back to that seemingly pre-recorded line of negative thought. We can begin to tell ourselves, hey, I'm okay, I'm strong, I can do that!

But here's the thing – and we'll keep going deeper into this throughout this book. If we're in general not very aware of our own mental habits and inner ruminations, we remain a victim to our habitual self-putdowns. To become victors instead of victims, we must regularly train ourselves to become more self-aware. That's the magic trick. Only then can we take steps to change any unwanted patterns of thought and behavior. We must observe and catch our worry-voice, our self-critic – and tell it to kindly shut up so that we can ease up on ourselves, pay attention to what really matters in our life, and yeah, enjoy our shower and our walks. We need to develop the mental power to stop putting ourselves down, and instead direct our focus of attention toward present-moment immersion in life.

When you do this, suddenly you'll feel better – relief! And in the blessed silence that ensues in your mind, you can also spontaneously allow yourself to open up and listen to your deeper true authentic voice. You can focus toward your heart where you don't feel at all separate ... and right then you can connect with intuitive inspired realms that your complaining ego or inner critic doesn't even know exist.

You might feel that this all sounds almost impossible to actually accomplish. The self-critic and all your negative programming you developed in childhood is so ingrained! Many of us have spent decades trying to break free, to push beyond our inner prison and emerge into a truly fresh realm of life – and thus far failed.

I remember hearing an old fable, I think from Japan or China, about someone who was locked away in a prison with thick bars separating them from all the world outside their tiny prison cell. Their life felt hopeless. But then one day they turned around, and saw that they're already on the outside, looking in at the prison. All they needed to do all along was to look and see that they're already free! But notice what was required – they had to consciously shift their focus of attention elsewhere ...

It seems that we can't wipe out and eliminate from our minds the negative experiences and programs we picked up in childhood. Like the herpes virus, they're always lurking in the shadows, ready to spring forth. But what we can do is stop giving them attention, energy, light. And as we'll see, we can even come to accept them rather than chronically deny their existence. After all, our authentic self includes all of us – and negative patterns can heal and become a valuable aspect of our selves.

As Within ... So Without

Unfortunately, many people with strong inner critics end up habitually projecting judgment onto the people around them. I will be encouraging you to begin to notice when you yourself are reflexively judging someone, fixating on their supposed faults, putting them down rather than building them up. It's so important not to hold and pass on the critical posture of your parents and childhood community. Begin to recognize that judgmental voice inside you – and ask it to kindly be quiet so that you can converse at brighter levels.

Also – the next time you're talking to someone, watch a similar voice in your head that's always busy coming up with a sharp counter-argument, trying to figure out what to say next instead of fully listening to what the other person is saying. Step back from these constant judgmental and dominating thought-flows, and shift your attention to your core inner presence. Drop your attention down to your heart, quiet your ego defenses, and open up to experience something new.

And regularly ask yourself: Is your habitual stance in life to find community and work together, or to find fault, to divide and separate and fight people who disagree with you? We currently see entire societies doing the negative act – taking sides and fighting rather than working together for the common good. This is a dangerous sickness of humanity, and it has its roots again in early-childhood experience. When people in authority constantly push us down, we develop a sense of inferiority – we're just not good enough. And so we overcompensate for this negative programming by acting superior ourselves, putting everybody else down so we seem in contrast to be super good and valuable.

Let's be blunt about this. The inner critic is a narcissist, a know-it-all, a bully – and if not dealt with, a destructive tyrant.

Far too many of our political leaders fall into this category. They have lost their sense of cooperation, compassion and community integration, and compulsively grab onto power. And rather than just tolerating them, we must call their bluff and disrupt their chronic put-downs and take-overs. However, rather than feeling superior to them, we also need to continue healing our own selves of this negative mental programming.

Will We Humans Ever Learn?

Peace, compassion and cooperation are what hold societies together. Forgiveness, acceptance and mutual trust are the cement of successful communities. But everywhere around us we can see uptight selfish egos, feeling threatened and isolated, disrupting our local and national wellbeing. Ego dysfunction of the collective human mind is playing out daily on the world stage. Turn on the nightly news and you immediately observe society's self-centered anxious attacks on the good life.

All this violence, division, polarity, hostility, manipulation and authoritarian dominance – it can look very much like some evil negative force has taken over the minds of the populace. And the same basic dynamic has been in play throughout history. We humans seem very slow to learn, and our aggressive genes don't help at all. Deep down we know that hatred and aggression never do anyone any good. Spiritually we can sense directly that we are all an integral part of the same larger community. But the inner critic fights against any efforts to regain social harmony – it sees only danger, separation and competition, resulting in hostility and conflict.

We shouldn't wait for others to wake up to all this – or we might wait our whole lives for improvement. Each of us must accept responsibility for our own inner quality of life. Our sense of loneliness, hopelessness and alienation is clearly the ego's creation, in contrast to our sense of unity, harmony, creativity and truth that emerges from a far deeper interior realm. I don't mean to sound preachy about this – but I do feel the necessity to speak up and point toward better times.

But let's not use aggressive means to promote change. Many spiritual teachers speak of 'the death of the ego' as a goal to strive for, but that puts us in a violent stance. Instead, as mentioned before, my aim is to put the ego function of the mind in its rightful place. Let it run our executive problem-solving dimension where we need to analyze, plan and go into action to get something done. But let's also actively empower and trust our other dimensions. Let's tap regularly into our intuitive powers, focus on compassionate emotions, and also regularly just plain kick back and enjoy the moment.

The self-centered ego's trick is making you think you have no deeper qualities, no deeper personality. It wants to control your attention and operate in your life like a secret agent, controlling you 24/7. As long as you remain oblivious to its presence it has you in its grip, and renders the 'deeper you' powerless to rise to the fore.

Seen in another light, your critical ego's only goal is to continually maintain itself and its illusions. It has a vested interest in making sure you never discover that your ego identity is not the real you. Spiritual awakening includes realizing that your surface personality changes in every new situation. As you learn to empower your deeper self, your ego identity will naturally lose its numbing grip on your higher consciousness.

Ultimately the aim of coaching is to help you gain a more expansive and realistic sense of who you really are – so you can escape the confinement of ingrained illusions about yourself, and relegate your ego function to tasks it can harmoniously take responsibility for. This is what is meant by developing an integrated personality. The various parts of your inner consciousness need to be brought together consciously into a broader, fully inclusive sense of self.

Seeking Deep Freedom

From my experience, our true self does in fact lie beyond our ego identity. Our individual consciousness is, in spiritual terms, 'one with' the ultimate infinite Consciousness that created the universe ... and beyond. It's often said that our personal identity is somehow grounded in the image and likeness of the Source, the Creator, God or whatever name we prefer to use for the divine essence of our souls. Each of us develops our own way of thinking about this universal truth, but everyone who looks deeply seems to arrive at the same inner realization: we're all in spiritual truth united and one. Therefore logically our ego-identity as a separate isolated entity is a very complex and potent mental illusion.

The Bible and many other religious texts often talk about there being an external devil that's trying to steal our souls – and indeed, when a self-centered neurotic ego has taken over someone's personality and sense of who they are, their soul does seem to get lost in the process. Life coaching for me, along with its more mundane pragmatic intentions, involves helping people get beyond selfish separating beliefs, and tap into the deeper spiritual dimensions of life.

And I repeat – as we rediscover our true essential self, the ego's illusions and distortions will step by step drop away, and in place of them we can begin to see reality itself more clearly. It's very much like waking up from a deep slumber. Who we really are has always been there, but it got pushed down and covered up in childhood by the ego's fear-based dominance.

So, is our challenge to make a complex effort to somehow escape ego dominance? I think not. In fact, just the opposite – we don't need to 'do' anything at all in order to connect with our deeper nature. All we need to do is relax, put aside our ego blinders that separate us from who we really are – and live more spontaneously in each new moment.

You know full well how thoughts are continually popping into your mind, seemingly out of nowhere. It seems very difficult to actively silence these thoughts – but hold in mind ... you don't have to attach your attention to them and therein feed them. Instead you can step back a bit, witness your thoughts, effortlessly observe them – but don't react or fixate on them. If you give them no attention, then almost as if by magic they'll fade and disappear from your awareness. Use mental judo in order to sidestep negative thoughts and emotions.

As Morpheus said in the film *The Matrix*:

> *You have to let it all go, Neo.*
> *Fear, doubt and disbelief –*
> *free yourself from Mind.*

Do you actually have a true inner voice of wisdom, insight, cooperation and communion with your higher self? The answer to this question will never be found in the cognitive thinking mind. In all spiritual traditions, our true inner voice speaks to us from our hearts, not our minds. We 'know' an insight or voice of guidance is true when we feel its veracity and power resonating in our hearts.

If you know deep in your heart that you are much more than the sum of your molecules and synapses, then no matter what your inner critic might say, you know in your heart and soul that you are vastly more than the sum of your parts. Many people are afraid that they might think an inner voice is real and to be trusted – but in fact it's their ego voice fooling them ... or worse, it's some evil voice of the devil fooling them. Throughout this book we're exploring how to become more astute about which voice you're hearing. It's vital to begin discerning who's talking to you or at you. You can actively begin to learn how to tell a nagging remnant of your father's judgmental voice from an inflow of authentic spiritual insight.

A number of therapy techniques envision a neurotic ego as a parasite or leech that's living in your energetic mind and sucking your life force to maintain its existence. Your ego actually has no material substance of its own, it's a cognitive creation – so it must of necessity live upon your authentic bodily and spiritual presence. And this 'sucking' reduces your overall power to grow and expand, and liberate your heart and soul from neurotic patterns.

A recent set of psychological studies demonstrate that being caught up in worries predictably fogs the mind, reduces our ability to think clearly, and saps our available energy. The research also documents that we can't be creative or relate with empathy when we're gripped by anxiety or depression. The downsides of harboring a neurotic ego are many – and the upsides of breaking free from your inner critic are truly liberating.

The neurotic ego's greatest fear is that we'll wake up and realize we don't need a fear-based fantasy presence ruling our lives. Perhaps we should feel pity for our inner critic, because it's in reality a frightened negative spirit that lives constantly in fear of its own annihilation. Because it thinks there is nothing at all beyond its isolated existence in your mind, it is deathly afraid you'll discover its illusory nature, and stop feeding its parasitic presence within you. It fears death itself, and therefore it will do almost anything to distract and thwart your efforts. That's why this challenge of healing the mind of its neurotic fears can seem so difficult to achieve.

This is a primary motivation for many of us seek a guide or coach, priest or therapist to help us maintain our intention of purging ourselves of a parasitic mindset that's determined never to surrender and fade into the background. It keeps us focused on the negative – and this in turn keeps us focusing our attention on exactly what we want to be free of.

CONCLUSION

Start to observe the neurotic aspects of your ego and see it for what it is. When you put the spotlight of your attention on it, you begin to gain control over your own mind. You gain autonomy in your own life. You decide, you choose. You take control. So, regularly start to tune into the still small voice within, and let the voice of your intuition lead the way. More and more, you'll find that your intuition is your only true compass in life. Learning to trust your own deeper self is perhaps the primary step in a fulfilling life.

What you 'see' is decided by who you put in charge of seeing. Is the ego your lookout, taking care of you – or is there a higher, wiser, more positive spirit overseeing your actions? I have found, when I go into the silence and tap into my intuition, that it never leads me astray. My intuition always points me toward the next step, and then the next.

CHAPTER TWO

How We Save The World

~~~~~~~~~~~~~~~~~~~~~~~~~~~~~

One does not become enlightened
by imagining figures of light
but by making the darkness conscious.

Carl Jung

As concerned individuals, most of us would like to be able to do something to make the whole world safer, less violent, more harmonious and joyful. But in almost every country, communities are drowning in misinformation, racial hatred and irrational rage. The collective mind of humanity, which is basically the sum of all individual minds taken together, seems to remain caught up in a mean, heartless, even soulless contraction. What's going on? Is all of humanity fatally gripped in a universal antagonistic neurosis? And what can we do about this deadly dilemma?

Carl Jung talked about there being an all-encompassing collective mind he called the collective unconscious, where each of us is an integral part of a non-material conscious whole. Recently astrophysicists and neurobiologists have generated science-based models for how each of us is constantly influencing the overall consciousness of the world. As Einstein said, everything influences everything. And that's the basic premise of quantum mechanics where scientific and spiritual models of the universe seem to finally be merging.
~~~~~~~~~~~~~~~~~~~~~~~~~~~~~

What this 'everything influences everything' means is that each of us is in essence personally responsible for the state of the world. When we let irrational neuroses run our own lives, we're also broadcasting negativity into humanity's collective unconscious. So ... to change our collective reality it's logical – we need to start healing and expanding our individual presence in the world. We need to foster more heart-centered awareness, and steadily tone down our fear-based fixations. Said another way: the main path for healing this confused and conflicted planet is to reduce our own anxiety and hostility, and take responsibility for our own life expression.

The Buddha's message 2500 years ago was: WAKE UP! The word 'Buddha' means 'awakened' or 'that which has become aware'. In each moment we're either less aware or more aware. Our quality of awareness fluctuates based on how we're managing our focus of attention – right now! And let's always remember – awareness contracts with pain and fear, and expands with harmony and joy. This means that if we want to become more aware, we must reduce our chronic emotional suffering. Instead we need to welcome and nurture the brighter thoughts that pop into our heads, and stop fixating on perpetuating the dark painful ones.

Eckhart Tolle in his book *The Power of Now* talks about this in terms of 'the pain body'. All children encounter pain and suffering – it's an inevitable aspect of life for all of us, like it or not. And Buddha identified the primary human dilemma as being stuck in chronic suffering. Only when we awaken deep-down, only when we transcend the thoughts that generate emotional suffering in our bodies, can we move beyond our suffering.

Every emotional pain that you experience leaves behind a wound that lives on inside you. This accumulated pain is a negative energy field that occupies your body and mind – it's an invisible entity in its own right. In fact it can't be separated from a neurotic ego that, as we've seen, is alive and intelligent – and can overwhelm the rest of you. But in reality it's a phantom, and can't prevail against the light of your spiritual presence.

When you fall into dark negative moods, this is the wounded emotional body in operation. You must become the witness of this process – just begin to observe it in action as it grabs you and pulls you down into suffering. As we saw in chapter one, the main tool or weapon you can employ to escape from a downer mood is your power of attention – but most people have not yet assumed full control of this power.

Also – our attention itself is under attack in our digital society. We now have a crisis of our collective attention. Fifty or even twenty-five years ago, there were no smart phones. Our moment-to-moment attention was mostly focused outward into the world around us, and we were free to focus in relative leisure where we wanted to. Our minds were relatively quiet and balanced. We could think things through, and often enjoy visual and audio pleasure and peace.

Now almost all of us are glued to our mobile phones or some related screen engagement. The commercial goal of all screen programming is basic: to hold your attention as long and as thoroughly as possible. Rather than being heads-up and present in the here and now, we're being pulled constantly off into quite questionable programmed experiences. Kids who from very early on have had a mobile phone in their hands have had their eyes so glued to this alternate reality that their brains are actually growing into quite different functions than ever before. And ... we're all being pushed further and further away from knowing how to be present, and how to wake up to discover our true selves.

This worldwide development seems unavoidable, and in many ways I love what tech is doing *for* us. But I cannot be supportive of what tech is doing *to* us. And if we don't wake up to this rapid universal spin into media nowhere-land, we're liable to end up becoming heartless biorobots with our brains continually being programmed by seriously questionable corporate entities.

But again – we can't just form a protest and fight against this subtle tech takeover. First we need to learn how to control where we choose to focus our personal attention. Then the light of our free spirits can shine on what's happening to our children's minds – and deal with the problem from a more-awake activist posture. We can radiate outward our creative energy, and change the world one person at a time.

Focused Attention Is Everything

It can't be said often enough: everything in our life is determined by where we focus our attention moment to moment. So our first challenge is to witness our own attention habits. Start to very clearly observe just how and where your attention is being distracted and gobbled up, moment to moment. And begin to evaluate the value to you of fixating your attention in media directions. What are you really getting out of it all?

To be quite honest, what you're getting out of your media distractions every day is self-stimulation. Media inputs are designed to provoke certain hormonal secretions that you naturally crave. It's almost the same as masturbation – and it's addictive. We're being manipulated by SMS, WhatsApp, Facebook, Instagram, TikTok, Emails, YouTube, Netflix, etc. We are being constantly distracted and interrupted. We might be focused on something important in our lives – but then the phone beeps incoming SMS, Email, WhatsApp message, and we switch our attention – because we hope we'll get a rush from the incoming.

Also, we're constantly switching from one media input to another, rather than learning to focus long enough on one thing to really get into it. This is accurately labelled 'invasive technology' because it's designed to grab our attention away from what we need to focus on.

We're actually being formally hypnotized by the media. Important research done after the second world-war demonstrated that there are two forms of hypnosis. There's the usual technique of slowing down a person's attention into a trance state, and then introducing a hypnotic condition – but there is also what's called hyper-hypnosis where you speed up auditory or visual information so fast that people lose their usual ability to think, to discern, to choose for themselves where they're going to focus their attention.

Hitler of course was the great hyper-hypnotist. We've all heard his speeches – his super-fast talking that induced a trance-like state of mass suggestibility. And notice that his rise to power coincided with the advent of the radio, where he could use hyper-hypnosis to program and motivate a large population. And now, notice how fast the media edits its content-shifts – faster and faster, to where the media user goes often into a trance-like state and absorbs the media input without discernment or reflection.

In my coaching work, one of the first essential steps with a client is to consider together their media usage and habits. If they want to become more conscious and successful, they simply must begin observing to what extent their attention has already been distracted and taken over. Only then can they begin the deeper process of purposefully choosing where they really want to focus their most precious resource.

Attention, focusing on a point, is always selective. What do we want to allow into our minds and hearts, to become part of our expanding sense of who we are? If we focus on violent heartless media inputs, we're basically programming ourselves with this killer aspect of human engagement – and we'll become more violence-prone ourselves. Therefore we must consciously look at what media we're absorbing, and ask ourselves seriously if we want to become that sort of person.

Our ego presence loves the news, it loves soaking up all the negative information. Even a healthy ego feels it needs to stay heads up about negative threats out there – but this becomes neurotic if it continually pushes our anxiety-buttons. Consuming the news often induces worry and even the feeling of panic. Watching the soaps generates misery through constrictive drama. It's important to remain present and observe what the shows are saying to you between the lines. See how you are being hypnotized, and watch out for the undertones of the program.

It's a statistical fact: around 90% of the news is negative and the undertone is danger, terror and worry. Are you ever in great form after watching the news? Stay present in front of the TV, observe and recognize what subliminal thoughts are being put into your mind. I suspect we never grow and feel better by watching the news and reading tabloids. If we look at the word Television, it's Tell a Vision (whose vision?) and they name what we watch Programs – yes, we're indeed being programmed. So we should be selective in what we choose to watch and let into our minds.

A valuable intention is to bring diversity to the content we consume. Is it wise to constantly consume the same media content delivered by the same people bombarding us with only one side of the argument? How can we ever open our mind to other people's perspectives if it's always filtered through the same forum. Don Miguel Ruiz in his book *The Fifth Agreement* states: "Be skeptical but learn to listen, because most of what you hear isn't true." Being skeptical is masterful because it uses the power of doubt to discern the truth. He also says be aware that most of humanity believes in lies, because there are two sides of all arguments. If we only hear one side of any argument, we are limiting our ability to see above and beyond our own viewpoint.

Awareness Is Our Tool

Humans are the only chronically-unhappy creatures on Earth, and this unhappiness is not our natural state. An ever-present timeless sense of well-being is the natural state of humans and animals alike. Just observe nature, it is our greatest teacher. We need to align our lives with nature. An animal can experience fear in a moment of attack – but shortly afterwards it settles back into its balanced blissful natural state. The cows and sheep in the fields aren't being interrupted all the time, they're munching grass, enjoying the sheer fact of being alive.

There is a perpetual calmness, a stability, a security in nature. Did you ever see a depressed horse or a sad flower? The feeling of well-being that you had in the womb – you were in paradise, you were fully taken care of. And most toddlers outside of war zones, before the development of their emotional body, live in a world of present-moment bliss before they get programmed with anxiety and pain by the world. They were in a bubble of love, they felt happy, alive and free. And this is still the essence of who you really are. This is your natural state when the ego isn't dominating.

What we are aware of we are in control of. What we are not aware of is in control of us. If we are not aware that we have an ego, if we are consumed by this dimension of our mind, then guess what – our ego is controlling us – and if it's neurotic it's ruining our otherwise-fulfilling life. The ego is like a DJ in our mind, playing the same song over and over again. And this repetition of the same old worry themes deadens the spirit. Thus we must learn to say – enough of this!

Whenever you catch yourself repeating nagging negative thoughts, shake them off at once. Refuse to be dragged down. And most important, choose wisely where to aim your attention in the next moment. When you wake up to the supposed battle in your ego-head, then the war in your head is over. And when you win the war in your head, you change your world. Sometimes when I'm in the shower and all this ego rubbish is running through my mind, I just shout out loud CANCEL, DELETE, SHUT UP. I tell it I am in charge and I choose right now to focus elsewhere.

This is the inner act of coming off automatic and becoming a connoisseur of your own thoughts. You are choosing not to get caught up in all the negative bullshit of your ego's mental mind chatter. Keep reminding yourself that the more aware you are, the less control your ego has over your thoughts. When you're in a bad mood, just pause and witness the mental activity in your mind – and you'll find that your mood begins to improve. Tune into your heart and wholebody feelings, and stop giving energy to your head's bothersome ruminations that are dragging down your mood.

It does take time and patience to do this kind of work. In this new age of technology, as I mentioned, we are bombarded all the time, our precious attention is being robbed from us in each media moment. And this means that we will need to consciously create open space and free time where we can witness what's happening in our minds, get in touch with ourselves, and listen to our deeper voice without constant external interruption. We must allow our heart, not our ego, to rule our life.

It seems that the ego function of the mind has little or no real connection to the heart's needs and wisdom. This is why the ego is the greatest obstacle to the inner healing process. Without a connection to our deeper heart-centered truths, the ego falsely believes that our suffering is caused by others. And the ego is therefore convinced it must defend itself against everything and everyone. When we experience suffering, it's always someone else's fault.

Next time you get triggered by what somebody calls you or does to you – ask yourself this question. What am I defending? You'll usually find that it's the ego's false image that you are defending. In reality the truth needs no defense – but the ego holds a false image of itself and therefore must fight back. We all have our imperfections and if we accept them, then the ego's false front becomes unnecessary.

If someone calls me a liar, I can find that somewhere inside me. Okay. If someone calls me a failure, okay, I can find it. Call me weak, I can agree. The recognition of the truth within me is a healing process. I am whole. I am okay. No need to argue or defend myself. The major source of satisfaction for the ego is proving that it's right and everyone else is therefore wrong. When we are defensive we have let the ego take charge.

The ego wants to fight and win, to be right and therefore to control. So when our ego encounters other egos, arguments result and we find ourselves getting defensive. The ego lives to attack. Blasting the horn at a driver who pulls out in front of us, yelling at our partner for being late, criticizing a child for doing something wrong or poorly – this may give us short term ego satisfaction. We're right and they're wrong. We get to feel righteous. But when we respond negatively to any situation we let our ego take charge. The ego loves to keep us tense and agitated, it loves stirring up trouble. All of this makes the ego feel essential, in charge, dominant. And ... as a result, our inner peace is shattered. Few of us would admit to preferring agitation over inner peacefulness – but we seem to do this over and over each new day.

Loving Our Whole Self

Everything in the manifest universe seems to consist of complementary opposites. In an atom, there is the proton and its opposite, the electron. Nature is essentially in balance energetically – and this is true inside our own minds. It's the ego that says, well, I'm definitely that but I'm definitely not that. I'm good, I'm not evil. But in fact each of us embodies both sides of a quality. We're good and yet sometimes we're bad. We're strong and yet sometimes we're so weak. We're smart but often we seem so dumb!

Every time you identify a negative quality in someone that you don't particularly like, pause for just a moment and see if you contain in some way that same negative quality within you that you're judging in the other person. If you can't see it within yourself, it's probably because you have repressed that quality. Your ego refuses to accept that it's not perfect. That can be a positive or negative quality.

We can all at times be strong or be weak, act responsibly or irresponsibly, be angry or loving, kind or cruel. When we can own all these qualities, we gain a newfound sense of balance and wellbeing – and this inner balance will impact the world around us. And life is an echo. What we send out, does surely come bouncing back. What we give – we receive. What we see in others exists also in us.

I like to see my own mind as a servant. Its reason for existing as an integral part of my whole being is to serve my higher good, and the good of my family and community. And it's my job to never allow my ego mind to run my whole life. And this means that if I find that my ego has become overly-dominant, my job is to learn how to put an end to my ego's rule. I want to lead with my heart, not my ego. And I want my soul to serve the greater spiritual good rather than being subsumed and buried.

Here's a challenge I give to you: Get set up and take ten to fifteen minutes to sit and record yourself – give yourself permission to say whatever comes to mind, with zero censorship or self-editing of what is flowing spontaneously into your mind. Just let it all come spewing out with zero ego constraint. Instead, let your ego show itself! I guarantee you'll be amazed at the amount of rubbish that comes spewing forth, the same type of rubbish that fills your head and keeps you occupied 24/7.

Also I challenge you to sit down and just write spontaneously for half an hour about whatever springs to mind, even if it's gibberish. You will perhaps be shocked to discover that you seem to have some nutter in there running the show. In *The Artist's Way* Julia Cameron talks about doing a morning writing meditation on a daily basis. I do this also, a brain dump that gets out into the open all the garbage and wisdom that's in your mind. By writing it down, somehow you get rid of the psychological luggage you woke up with. And after you write down what's lurking in your subconscious basement that morning, you don't need to read over it and evaluate it – just toss it away, and begin your day with a fresh open mind.

As mentioned earlier, when the ego mind lets go of its frantic struggle to comprehend and dominate, and falls silent for even a few moments, we can begin to tune into our deeper guiding voice that's been waiting to reach us all the time. When the ego's voice is absent, our inner self will inspire us, often in silence, toward a certain action or direction that resonates with our higher creative being.

Hold in mind that this inspiration doesn't usually come in auditory words or thoughts. Each of us taps into our inspired guidance in our own way. When the ego's voice has died down and there is peace and silence, your true inner self is ready and eager to take your hand and move you gently toward valued expression.

You can take the exercise of writing down the garbage that is filling your mind, and apply it to receiving valued insights. This is an entire process in and of itself for tapping creative inflows. When you learn to feel quiet and peaceful and receptive inside, you can sit and breathe and allow Spirit by whatever name to gently and often deeply speak to you through spontaneous writing.

You may feel confused at times as to whether such inspiration is coming from the ego or the still small voice deeper within, but don't worry. If you stay tuned into your heart, you'll soon learn to discern your ego voice from your true voice. This is an ability I always help my clients develop. It's mostly a feeling in the heart. If it's your inner guide then something bubbles up brightly within you. And it's not an effort – it's just the opposite. It's a gift, a discovery, a helping hand.

The ego voice usually has a sense of urgency to it, whereas the voice of Spirit is much gentler. The still small voice is calm while the ego is hectic and fear-inducing. The voice of Spirit is rational and wise while the neurotic ego jumps to false conclusion. Also, I find that Spirit's voice is quiet, while the ego voice is loud. And most important, Spirit's voice is loving while the ego voice is dominating. And finally, the still small voice responds while the ego's voice reacts.

The Bible states this perfectly:

Be still ... and know that I am God.

Who's In Charge Here?

Beyond your front door, beyond your job, beyond your relationship, beyond the screen is a world full of discovery. You will never realize your potential unless you go out, or rather go in, and look for it. Too often we rely on second-hand knowledge, especially about our own inner workings. We need to go within and discover for ourselves the normally-hidden layers that lie just below our surface. There is so much more to us than we can ever imagine.

We think we know ourselves, but we are living in a picture of our own creation. What we see and experience is a reflection of our own minds. Our world is literally our mirror, it reflects back to us our own mental state. And too often this state is seeing everything that's happening in our lives as happening TO us rather than happening FOR us.

When we see things as happening to us, what we see is a world full of accidental happenings. And when we resist what's happening, we think life is not as it should be. However, when we are truly aligned with reality, we begin to see there are no mistakes. We begin to understand that what we see is always a reflection of our own beliefs and expectations. And with this perspective, we are able to converse with a living intelligence.

Most people think that their thoughts and feelings arise from or are caused by external events, people and circumstances. I might assume that the rude shop assistant made me angry, a cancelled flight generated my frustration, or conversely walking by the sea made me feel calm. Seeing life this way makes it appear that our thoughts and feelings originate from outside ourselves. And this implies that external events and people have power over us – the power to stimulate our feelings and emotions.

That could not be further from the truth. If you assume that your thoughts and emotions originate from external circumstances then your focus of attention will go toward changing the circumstances. Then trying to make those changes will cause further discomfort. Without an appreciation of how your mind works, you can waste a lot of energy ruminating about and then perhaps acting to change external situations over which you might have no control. Thus you assume and create your own negative reality.

The psychological reality is that the suffering we feel is not dependent upon outside events or people – no one but ourselves can create what we feel inside. Two people can have an identical experience and yet respond with totally different feelings. The reason we don't escape our suffering and frustration when we leave a relationship or change careers or leave the country is that suffering is internal and we take it with us wherever we go.

As the old Zen saying goes – wherever we go, here we are. Our suffering is caused by the negative energy patterns we are holding within us, not by anything else. Our ongoing reality emerges from inside us. And until we take charge of our internal reality we will keep re-experiencing whatever is stored in our ego mind and emotional body.

That which you do not make conscious
comes around to meet you as fate.
That which you resist you draw to you.
Resistance creates persistence.
That which is denied stays around.

Carl Jung

So many people believe in accidents, random events or unexplained illnesses – they attribute them to hard luck, fate, chance, or being in the wrong place at the wrong time. But too often this attitude is an ego trick to remove ourselves from feeling any responsibility for what is happening. It leads us to believe that we are living in a world ruled by random chance. We then believe that events are meaningless or pointless. But when we wake up to see reality as it truly is, in essence and in scientific fact we live in an orderly universe. There is an underlying structure and order to everything – it's not random chance that the butterfly emerges from its chrysalis and takes flight, or that the acorn becomes an oak tree.

Look at the intelligence in the human body – how an embryo forms and develops within the womb into a fully grown baby. All of this is being done by the incomprehensible perfection of life itself. Look everywhere in nature and you will see this order, this perfect structure, this integrated intelligence. Go out on a clear night and look up at the stars, or watch a sunrise or sunset or the beautiful perfectly-ordered colors of a rainbow.

Likewise we're a tiny integral part of a vast limitless consciousness and divinely ordered universe. Our body breathes without assistance on our part. Our heart beats all on its own all day long, blood circulates through our veins and arteries to every part of our body. All the various life-sustaining systems in our body – our circulation, breathing, blinking, swallowing, eating – are perfectly synchronized by an intelligence that operates far beyond our ego mind. And our own individual life has structure and order to it as well.

Meaning And Purpose

Show me your thoughts and I will show you your life. The Inner always determines the Outer. If you were typing an email and you misspelled a word, the error started in your mind and then appeared on the email. If you look to the source of the error, and in extension to the source of your suffering, you'll find that your life isn't just some random mistake or the fault of some external person or situation. Your life is not what it is today because of all your seemingly-accidents, losses, traumas and so forth. There has always been a larger order to your flow of life, quietly seeking to emerge.

In my understanding, no one is where they are now by accident. Life is like a divine tapestry, and each thread is vital to the overall picture. I feel that we were born into our particular family for a reason and a purpose. Our family is our greatest teacher. And every member of one's family will hold at least one trait we don't like. Conversely, we will have at least one trait that family members dislike. Our family is like our childhood class room for our emerging life.

In Louise Hay's book *You Can Heal Your Life*, she goes one step further and suggests that quite possibly we somehow choose our particular set of parents because they will mirror the pattern or gift we are bringing into the world. She feels that we have come here to learn a particular lesson and talent that will advance us on our spiritual pathway, and be of value to humanity. For our Western view of life this might seem a bit esoteric but I find deep value in this perspective.

As you consciously join the dots of your life, you'll begin to see the overall pattern and how it all connects. Your life does have meaning and purpose, there is a definite design to it, a particular theme. And I encourage you to clarify your life story so you can interpret and uncover the message, the meaning, and the overarching direction your life thus far is pointing you in. This is a major aspect of my coaching process. Like a jigsaw puzzle, you can put the pieces of your life together to see what larger picture is now emerging.

I deeply believe that existence needs each of us. Without our unique contribution, something in existence will be missing – our piece of the jigsaw puzzle. If we don't get clear, step up and manifest our role in the fabric of life, there will be a place vacant which cannot be filled by anyone except ourselves. Each of us is intimately related to existence. Existence has brought us here, we have some special destiny to fulfill through our presence and our actions – and this is where we find true satisfaction in life. So I encourage you to focus intently on uncovering your real reason for being here.

Your life is like a treasure hunt – there are clues along the way, all of which point toward the hidden treasure, clues everywhere if you choose to look. There is indeed order in the universe. And one of the big benefits of joining the dots of your life story is that you begin to heal your story. When you put the jigsaw pieces of your life together and see the bigger picture, your life starts to make sense.

In this self-reflective process you will begin to realize the high level of creativity and productivity you uniquely possess. You begin to see how the 'enemies' in your life have actually been allies in a bigger plan, guiding and often provoking you toward your destiny. Yes, on the surface it might look like everything is just random chance and accidental – but underneath it all, there is a definite plan.

Like a jigsaw puzzle, in your life there are thousands of pieces, all different shapes and sizes. And for every person in your life this is also true. Your job and opportunity is to fulfill your unique role in the universal puzzle. Once you gain clarity about your life story, you'll find that your piece will fit perfectly and harmoniously with all the other pieces.

Just being yourself is the greatest gift you can give. When you only see your life through the filter of your ego wounds you can get trapped in your story. But when you look at it from a higher and deeper level, obstacles become opportunities, struggles serve to make you stronger, and enemies become allies. Your deeper life purpose is encrypted into your life story. With a bit of honest reflection, you can begin to see why things have happened as they did.

When we all contribute our unique valuable piece of the life puzzle, then the perfect picture can emerge. For instance, I had two very self-absorbed parents, and as a result they never listened to me – family life was all about them. And after years of never been listened to, I emulated their behavior. I didn't listen to myself. This is a basic psychological fact: we tend to treat ourselves the way others have treated us. I was in essence caught in a life trap of subjugation, people-pleasing and just going along with what others wanted, as opposed to following my intuition and doing what I felt moved to do.

I then started to wake up and heal my wounds. I started tuning into my intuition and listening to myself. What I found was that I wasn't happy in my career, so I got clear on what I wanted. I had done business studies because that is what my friends were doing at the time and I just went along with them. I ended up working in finance, which I hated. When I started listening to my gut, I chose to go back to school and study psychology which came so natural to me. I became a psychotherapist, then years later I also studied the emerging profession of Life Coaching. I now combine the two.

In retrospect I can see that the negative childhood experience of not being listened to eventually led to me breaking free and listening to myself – and then listening deeply to others. Thus the negative 'given' of my parents was transformed into an important positive in my life. I am a very good listener in my therapy work and an effective mediator in couples coaching. People pay me to listen to them but it doesn't feel like work to me, I now love what I do. I've discovered that I am a natural peacemaker and that makes me a good mediator. I can listen without judgment, and create space for everyone to air their grievances, needs and aspirations.

I feel that I'm now in the exact right career for me, my work is a joy and I'm using my signature strengths in my job. And naturally this is what I help my clients to also strive to attain. I love this related quote:

The secret of success is to
make your vocation your vacation.

Mark Twain

It's often risky to take the leap and give your life fully to what you love most, what moves you and brings you joy and fulfillment. But it's definitely worth it, because the opposite of this is having a comfortable, safe, predictable life which has no comparison to feeling passionately alive each and every day.

When I listen with empathy to my clients I know I am giving them psychological air, so to speak. I listen with empathy, and this allows the person to expose their core problem, and discover a solution at their own pace, layer by layer. Again – through connecting the dots in my family of origin, I now get to do the job that I am excellent at. Listening was missing in my family so that is what I was called to bring.

I have two siblings who were born deaf, my older brother and my younger sister. From growing up with them I have also step by step learned the art of interpreting body language and listening to what people are not saying, which is quite important for a therapist or coach to pay attention to. In essence I've learned to listen to the whole person and not just the words that come out of their mouths – the nonverbal and usually unconscious forms of communication. Deep within our humanness is a profound need to be heard and understood as a whole person. A life coach provides the opportunity to truly be heard – and also teaches clients how to listen to themselves.

Imagine that you have listened to your deeper needs, and are now doing what you love most. Imagine that you're giving your best to the people around you, and they're thankful to benefit from what you offer. This is a most wonderful feeling. You're being responsible, accountable, you're no longer being selfish, no longer keeping yourself small and contracted when many people could benefit from your talents and gifts. Instead you're responding to your unique life challenge, and you're finding meaning in everything you do. You're re-engaged with your life.

Assuming responsibility empowers us. When we refuse to take accountability we lose the chance to empower ourselves, and also the chance to get out in the world and learn important lessons. We end up missing out on so much. It's so important to accept full responsibility for all that happens in our lives.

No matter what external issue my clients feel moved to talk about, I always get them to look at what part they themselves played in the scenario. Blaming other people gets us nowhere. We cannot change other people, and external situations are usually difficult to transform. As I say over and over, the only person we can change is ourself. And when we transform our own thoughts and actions, this will generate a domino effect on others in our life.

When I worked in the area of domestic violence I found that a lot of the women I was supporting were habitually waiting on Him to change his abusive ways – all their focus was on Him. I used to patiently point out to them that the only person they have the power to change is themselves. I would step by step help them to shift their attention away from Him and what he was doing or not doing, and focus on empowering themselves.

For instance I would teach them how they could discern the interpersonal traits of safe versus unsafe people. As statistics show, abused people have the tendency to fall into certain patterns of choosing to get involved with hurtful abusive people over and over again. I observed that far too many women would leave an abusive relationship, only to enter another abusive relationship. I would get these women to identify red flags when meeting new people, as a key strategy in empowering themselves against bad relationship-choices in the future. In the context of abusive relationships, red flags are like warning lights saying slow down and pay attention.

CONCLUSION

Your world without is a reflection of your world within. When I began to look within and make changes for the better, I found that my outer world followed suit and began to reflect the inner changes. When my inner world changed, my outer world naturally changed too. As within so without.

Life has always been reflecting your 'inner game'. So use this to your advantage.

CHAPTER THREE

Exploring Your Childhood

~~~~~~~~~~~~~~~~~~~~~~~~~~

Give me the child till he is seven years old
and I will show you the man.

Old Jesuit Saying

As this quote shows, the first six years of our lives determine so much of what's to come. Infants and toddlers are living sponges, they naturally absorb the outside world – and this includes the emotions, attitudes, prejudices and all the rest that can be picked up from parents, siblings and extended family.

That's why it's so important to look back and study our personal history in order to understand our lineage, and then to evolve it. When I do enquiry into a client's family history, a lot of clients say: "I can't blame my parents." I spend a lot of time explaining that this work is not to blame parents – but it is necessary to clarify our lineage and unravel what happened in our childhood – and also to consider the impact our childhood still has on our adult lives.

We can't eradicate the first decade of our lives, or ignore them as insignificant. I'm not saying that we will necessarily stay mired in our long-gone past. But we can learn to accept and integrate and also forgive the past, and then leave it where it belongs. No one can alter what happened – but we can surely
~~~~~~~~~~~~~~~~~~~~~~~~~~

transcend it. The old adage says it this way: *you don't know where you are going until you know where you've come from.*

Rather than a process of placing blame, unravelling family history is a way of becoming more aware of repeated family patterns so that we can then consciously make better choices in our own lives. I often have clients write out their current version of their family history. This version is always colored by the client's attitude toward their past – was it all rosy, all terrible, or something in-between? By writing it down, it's possible to gain perspective on our heritage and life story.

What can be seen to repeat over and over again in that story? And what does the client want the rest of their life story to include? What needs to now be faced, sorted out, and healed? How can negative patterns be discarded? What is the responsible act in the present moment that will empower this transformation?

The relationship between parent and child is of course the most complicated one a person will ever participate in. It's even more complicated than between wife and husband, partner and partner. Children from birth onward mimic and absorb what parents say and do. That's how our species survives. Our parents were our role models. How they treated themselves and how they treated us became the model for how we even now treat ourselves.

Even with mature adults there tends to be much unfinished business and unresolved conflicts in our relationship with our parents. There are many ways to deal with this, ranging from basic behavioral therapy to esoteric methodologies. Many spiritual circles believe we're born into a particular family for a purpose – to exasperate or magnify issues in our souls which need provocation in order to evolve. No one knows scientifically if reincarnation is a reality – but there is something true and important in this view of life.

At more psychological levels, so many people attempt as adults to unconsciously recreate the conditions of their upbringing, perhaps in order to correct and break free from them. They return to the scene of their original wounding in an attempt to resolve unfinished business. Often the problems between husband and wife or partner and partner stem from unresolved conflicts with one or both of their parents.

There's no question that a lot about our psychology as an adult is reflecting our childhood. Clients often ask how come they aren't the same as their siblings even though they were raised by the same parents. The answer is complex. Each child is genetically unique, first of all. And each parent treats each child differently. Also birth position is very important – a first child is treated very differently than a second child for instance.

Definitely, each child has a different temperament, and they interpret feelings and events in their own unique way. They develop quite different narratives of their family history. Many of my clients in the first few sessions tell me how they had a wonderful childhood, then a few sessions later the truth begins to emerge – they had far from wonderful childhoods, and were only being protective of their parents. I tell them this enquiry is not to lambast or blame their parents. Most parents did their best with the knowledge and temperament they had at the time. They did their best – but still the client was hurt and damaged as a child.

And logically this means that when you're in therapy or coaching, it's usually necessary to look openly at the impact that a childhood hurt had on you and your life. You have to be brave and find any hurts that might still be running your life. Examine all the significant people who had an influence in your childhood – parents, caretakers, step-parents, siblings, teachers, priests, scouts leaders, sports coaches. Don't judge them – just evaluate how they impacted you then, and how they might be still impacting your current life.

I don't think anyone emerges from childhood unscathed by emotional and attitudinal wounds. It all comes with the territory of being human, because there's no such thing as perfect parents, siblings, teachers and so forth – because there is no such thing as a perfect person, period. Freud said quite firmly that neurosis is the rule in society, not the exception.

Each of our lives is an ongoing drama because we're all imperfect and our imperfections generate conflict that begs resolution. Drama is all about damaged personalities. What therapy and coaching can offer is a chance to become the script-writer of the rest of your life. Keep all the good bits you inherited, and heal the not-so-good bits. The choice is always the same – chronically re-enact your past ... or step forward and rewrite the script for your future.

The wonderful spiritual teacher Ram Das said something like this: *When you think you have reached enlightenment, go spend a week in your parents' home.* When feelings from childhood are buried alive and repressed, they will fester and continue to seek expression until exposed and allowed to heal.

Resolving Traumas

My mother had NPD (Narcissistic Personality Disorder) and some of those traits include being very manipulative, emotionally unavailable, controlling and self-absorbed. My father was an alcoholic and absorbed in his addiction. As a child my emotions and needs were invisible – it was all about their needs, not mine.

I tended to attract a lot of narcissists, usually female just like my mother. I did a lot of healing work on the mother wound.

And I also had relationships with men who were emotionally unavailable, until I learned how to evaluate relationships and drop out of those that didn't serve me.

Healing our old emotional wounds is like peeling an onion layer after layer. I had a friend whose father was a roaring alcoholic, so she was determined not to marry a man that drank too much. But she picked a husband who rarely drank, but it turns out he was a workaholic. Instead of alcohol it was work – but with the same basic effect in the home. Father always in the pub = the absent father. Husband always in the office = the absent husband.

Trauma can be both quick and also long-term timewise. One violent experience can create long-lasting trauma effects. But equally, being caught in a toxic home environment for years can also result in serious PTSD effects. In both cases, the unconscious urge to resolve trauma through re-enactment can be severe and compulsive. Struck by the way in which people's entire lives could keep replaying themes from their childhood, Freud coined the term *Repetition Compulsion to* describe behaviors, relationships, emotions and dreams that seem to be replays of earlier trauma.

The motivation to re-enact early painful experiences can be seen as naturally seeking to heal a buried trauma by bringing the trauma to the surface so that unfinished grieving and healing can happen. People create new but similar pain so that they provoke the situation and feelings of an early pain, bring themselves out of an unconscious state, and hopefully complete the arrested healing process.

We often do need to go back to the origin and heal the wound at its source. One way or another we might need to re-experience what it was like for a child to never be listened to. Did it make them feel unimportant, that they were of no value or significance? And in similar circumstances as an adult, does a husband who often doesn't listen make the wife feel unimportant and of no value? Does a man who never got his father's approval end up an adult who's always almost pathetically trying to gain support and recognition from his spouse and his employer?

Our mammalian reaction to extreme danger or trauma is to play dead, to pass out, to go unconscious and thus avoid the whole situation. If we can't fight and overcome a threat (being shouted down or violated by parents in a toxic home environment for instance), and also if we can't run away from a bully or dangerous situation – what can we do? We can disappear inside. We can blot out the experience entirely, and let it fester inside us long-term.

I currently seldom deal with extreme trauma or violation cases, I leave that to the PTSD experts. But almost everyone I coach has had less-extreme traumatic experiences which need attention and resolution. They need to acknowledge the trauma, accept what happened – and often be guided back in memory to relive the trauma episode, often several times. Otherwise the trauma can block all other realms of emotional healing.

Evaluating Your Parents

We all agree that our childhood experience with our parents or caregivers deeply impacted who we are now as adults. But far too many people have avoided really looking closely at who their parents actually were. Therefore I often have my clients take an informal inventory of all the positive and negative traits of their mother and father. What were their parents' views on things like money, love, work, God, sex, children and so forth. And which of these traits has the client unconsciously imitated in adult life? Does the client ever catch themselves sounding just like their mother or father?

You might want to do this inventory yourself. Just read the following questions, and then on paper or a computer see what comes spontaneously to mind – and write down your reflections in as much depth as you want:

> *Are you still blindly following the basic way your parents did things?*
>
> *Have you advanced to where you can question their beliefs, their habits, their attitudes?*
>
> *What were the unspoken rules or injunctions passed on to you from your mother and father?*
>
> *What was the quality, honesty, mutual respect and emotional depth of your parents' relationship?*
>
> *How did they express love and handle all their various conflicts and emotions?*
>
> *What was their style of parenting – were they authoritarian or permissive?*
>
> *How did they handle conflict?*
>
> *How did they handle money?*
>
> *How where things resolved if there were disagreements?*
>
> *Did they respect and value each other, or did they take each other for granted?*

I remember that when my parents argued, my mother would go numb and do the silent treatment, not talking to my father for upwards of two to three weeks at a time. I recall during one of her silent episodes, siting in the living room with my dad, and my mother walked in and said to me, "Tell your father his dinner is ready." And too often when my dad smelled of drink and my mom complained, there would ensue an almost-violent angry outburst that deeply traumatized me. The result was that I avoided conflict like the plague in adulthood.

I am sure you have heard the story of Grandma's Ham. It's a story of a mother who always cut the ends off of her ham every Christmas. One Christmas day her daughter asked why she cut the ends off the ham and her reply was: "Oh, I don't know. My mother always cut the ends off of hers." So the daughter went to her grandmother and asked her why she cut the ends off her ham. The grandmother replied: "I don't know. My mother always cut the end off of hers." Finally the daughter went to her great-grandmother and asked her why she cut the ends off her ham. "Honey, back in the day we didn't have a pot big enough to hold the whole ham so I had to cut the ends off so the ham would fit in my pot."

A simple example in my own life is how we crack our soft-boiled eggs. When my husband and I boiled eggs for breakfast I would take my knife and slice the top off my boiled egg, while my husband would take his spoon and tap it on the top of the egg to crack the shell. I remember one day being in his father's house and his father was having a soft-boiled egg and he tapped the top of his egg with the spoon just like my husband did.

This simple gesture had been passed down without reflection. It was just how thing were done in his family, regardless of whether it was the best way. I recommend that you begin to question if you are blindly following the ways your parents did things. If you find that you have emulated their good traits and are using them in your life, then be grateful for all the good stuff they passed on to you. My mother deeply believed in getting an education – and I'm grateful to this day for that. I have good careers because of my mom in this regard. Another thing my mom believed in which has rubbed off on me is to never waste anything. She would boil a chicken and then make chicken stock with the boiled water. With left over bread she would make breadcrumbs and stuffing for the chicken.

I remember going to our neighbor who was a dressmaker with a red coat that was too big for my mother, asking the dressmaker to make two beautiful small red coats with the material from my mother's coat, for me and my sister. To this day I waste nothing. I always give away clothes that I no longer want to the charity shop.

But I also now know the negative traits of my parents that I took into my own life as an adult, and had to work considerably to become free of. In the process my inner narrative of my life story evolved considerably. I recommend this process to everyone. Don't blame your parents – take full responsibility for your current life. But do get clear on what really happened back then.

The Familiarity Principle

As we're exploring, our early relationship with our parents created a script or a model for how our future relationships would look like. People tend to choose romantic partners with traits similar to their parents. And sometimes when we look for partners who are as different from our father or mother as possible, our opposite choice is still in effect a decision conditioned by them – still a reaction rather than a conscious choice.

We are often drawn to people who feel familiar energetically because they fit our early family patterns. They are perhaps emotionally unavailable, addictive, maybe even abusive – and we are drawn to them because of unresolved childhood wounds. Said slightly differently, we are attracted to people whose emotional dynamic and condition is similar to our first experience of love. There is great, but often neurotic, power in this type of attraction. These people will match your childhood pattern – but watch out if this pattern is unhealthy. You might be recreating your original wounding, perhaps hoping to 'get it right' this time – but often just sinking blindly into another familiar dysfunctional relationship instead.

Of course if you had wonderful loving parents, finding a similar mate might work quite well. The relationship might be relatively easy and smooth and long-lasting. But what Freud called the repetition compulsion can ruin lives. When I'm doing couple counseling I come across this very often – and ultimately a lot of clients realize they married a version of one of their parents. We do repeat what we haven't repaired. Identifying behavior traits that are similar between one's spouse and a parent can be enlightening, and also encourage a healing process.

We might marry a neurotically-critical person like our father and push him to be more accepting – or a cold woman like our mother and try to make her warm. We search for an aloof distant man just like our dad and try to get him to commit to family life. I often ask this question of my clients: what happens if you squeeze an orange, what comes out of it? They say orange juice of course. I then point out that the reason orange juice comes out is because that's what's IN THERE.

Take road rage as an example. If someone cuts me off in traffic and I erupt with anger, the person cutting me off just 'squeezed' me and my anger came out of me because it was in there in the first place. When someone is bugging me and pushing my buttons, I might explode overmuch over some little thing because they're tapping an old wound that's under pressure to come out.

A sign of emotional maturity is when we can recognize this type of over-reacting scenario – and take the occasion to look deeply into the actual source of our explosion. Rather than blaming the person who provoked the explosive reaction we can thank them for exposing something that needs healing. And likewise, when a depressing or anxious emotion suddenly surfaces for no apparent reason, if we're honest with ourselves we can own the upset and take it as an opportunity to release that buried feeling in a healing way.

When something generates an over-strong emotional reaction in you, that's a trigger that you need to identify and watch for. It's unfair and damaging in a relationship to over-react. Maybe that over-reaction is familiar, maybe you've been doing it most of your life – but as an adult you're responsible for first controlling it, and then moving beyond it. Learn productive ways of responding when provoked. Get to know yourself when under stress. With a bit of practice you can trace your emotional reactions back to their origins, and deal with them appropriately.

Can you remember the first time you reacted inappropriately with an unwelcome emotion? I encourage you to start being an observer of yourself, become a detective in your own life. Ask questions like what am I feeling? Why did I react like that? What does this situation remind me of from my past? Why do I react the way that I do? Try to spot your own out-of-place emotions in books and movies. When a character from a movie or book sticks in your mind, there might be a parallel between the character and you. Seeing this can lead you in the right direction to healing the original wound.

Movies that make us emotional and perhaps cry a lot are usually ones that resonate at some level with the storyline of our own life. A movie can provide genuine healing and resolution because it does provoke a buried emotion that needs to come up and out. That's fairly obvious. Drama for thousands of years has been helping us get buried feelings exposed – in Greek it's called *catharsis*. And catharsis works best if we have an emotional release – and then take time to reflect on where that buried emotion originally came from. When you never stop to think about your upsurges of feelings and how they're too often influencing your behavior, you leave yourself set up to be hijacked by unwanted emotions over and over again. When such emotions are allowed to control you, you move through each new day dominated by your feelings with little choice in what you say and do. You stay stuck as a victim of your past.

An over-reacting emotion is a memory without words. It's a signal indicating that your body is still storing an earlier trauma that hasn't been fully released. Our conscious mind gains access to what our body still remembers of a trauma through the process of a usually-unwanted emotional upsurge. If and when we manage to listen to such an upsurge in the present moment, it can provide a direct link to what still ails us from the past.

Beyond Childhood Identities

A client of mine who was divorced was now having a very intense relationship with a man she was mad about. Then out of the blue he suddenly told her it was over. She was devastated – she admitted to me that she felt totally abandoned, and that this was something that had happened to her too often in her life. She had a whole section in her mental library called Abandonment. I helped her finally trace this recurrent issue back to her father who had suddenly walked out of her life, literally vanished forever when she was just eight years old. And ever since, it seemed that people kept doing this terrible thing to her.

My client had never processed and healed her feelings of abandonment when her father left, because she was trying to be strong in front of her mother. Finally in therapy, she was able to really cry and grieve for that little eight-year-old girl whose father had abandoned her. After the crying came anger and rage. During the early therapy sessions with me she tried to act like she wasn't an angry person at all – but I could hear the anger leaking out in our conversations, even though she seemed totally unaware of its presence.

Her anger at men in general was massive. Her recent heartbreak was a good opportunity for her to get in touch with that agony of hurt and betrayal that she still felt toward her father, and then toward the men in her life that she felt had also betrayed her. She had a strong habit of totally blocking recognition of this emotion inside her – but I told her it was healthy and healing to acknowledge and release her buried feelings.

Emotional release in a safe surrounding is so good for us – to let it all flow out, be seen, and then let go of. I encouraged her to feel free to cry and shout and scream and otherwise be free to express buried feelings in our sessions. I also encouraged her to go home and run up and down the stairs a few times growling and releasing anger – and also to really let go and scream in the house when nobody was there. I also encouraged her to get a pillow and bash it with an old slipper, beat the hell out of the pillow and get all of that anger that's inside out in the open. After all, anger is just a mental vomit that needs to come out. Doing something physical is a great way to encourage this.

Another safe place to release pressurized feelings is driving alone in the car – give yourself permission to let out a big scream when driving (with the windows up!). Using words for release is also effective. One woman who in general was unable to say no, found great help in shouting "NO!" over and over as she drove to work every morning. After a while she found that she was then able to say No in actual real-life situations.

After clients have physically released all the anger or other habitually-buried emotions inside them, they are then in a much calmer position to deal with the unresolved anger from their past. They can look honestly and find the message in the anger. Maybe they need to finally say "This is not fair" or "I need you to love me, not shout at me" or "I deserve better" or "Stop violating my private boundaries!"

Denying and suppressing negative feelings of any kind doesn't make that energy go away. So along with screaming out one's anger, I also urge clients to wail, to sob, to shake or whatever, to release all that suppressed energy their body is still storing. These denied emotions actually get buried alive in the body. And the really sad thing is that when we repress one emotion, we tend to repress all our emotions. If we block anger for instance, or grief, we can become emotionally cold in general. A heartless person is usually a heart-broken person.

We are supposed to feel. Our emotions are there for a purpose. When they flow freely, we're charged with the life force, we're vibrant and beautiful. But when a physically beautiful or handsome person blocks their feelings, they turn ugly. They broadcast the very emotion they're blocking. All of us need to get emotionally honest with ourselves – otherwise our repressed feelings explode outward in anger and violence, or implode inwards as depression, anxiety or illness.

I tell clients to pause and check in when they feel triggered by their partner, and ask a few simple questions of themselves:

What's the real source of this emotion?

Am I feeling like I did as a child?

What memory underlies this current unwanted feeling?

Who Are You Really?

There's a big difference between feeling *self-conscious* which means being bashful and worried about how people are seeing you, and being *self-aware* which means honestly observing and learning from your inner mental and emotional condition. Feeling self-conscious is grounded in insecurity and anxiety. Self-awareness is grounded in expansion and awakening. Between the stimulus and the response, we can take a deep breath, look beyond the present moment into our past, and notice the source of our present reaction. Then we can respond more appropriately in the present moment.

This self-aware stance is such an important part of a happy mature marriage. Rather than just automatically playing out a recurring conflict, we can observe that we're re-enacting scenarios from our past, and choose to let all the past go, so that we're fresh to relate in new ways. This aware stance holds the hope that this time we'll get it right and be free from the past.

Here's a rather blunt tongue-in-cheek poetic expression of how our childhood tends to make a mess of our adult lives:

THIS BE THE VERSE by Philip Larkin

They fuck you up, your mum and dad.
They may not mean to, but they do.
They fill you with the faults they had
And add some extra, just for you.

But they were fucked up in their turn
By fools in old-style hats and coats.
Who half the time were soppy stern
And half at one another's throats.

Man hands on misery to man,
It deepens like a coastal shelf.
Get out as early as you can –
And don't have any kids yourself.

You like everyone obviously have your life story that you carry along everywhere inside you. The origin of your story was almost certainly early in your childhood when you developed a core sense of your identity, your sense of self. This 'self' was a belief or survival mechanism that strived to make sense of your childhood experience – and it probably more or less served its purpose. You were immersed in a family circle, and you defined yourself based on that family dynamic.

But this budding identity-strategy is probably no longer applicable in your adult life. It was very wise of the child to adapt this self-defense strategy, but as an adult it's wise to drop the limited childhood stance in life, and open up to a broader, more enjoyable and creative sense of who you really are. This is a primary aim of coaching, as I see it.

For me, being invisible and fading into the woodwork kept me safe in my family of origin. There was enough chaos going on around me that being invisible was a very safe strategy. Subjugating and always doing things my mother's way definitely saved me a few clatters of the wooden spoon. I learned that the best way to keep harmony in my family was to 'disappear' and not cause anyone any trouble. I learned that if I was undemanding and had few expectations, in other words if I were a low-maintenance child, this would protect myself while calming down Mummy and Daddy. I thought that if I stay out of the way, the family would stay together. So I just tried to blend in as much as possible.

I remember one time buying a box of milk tray chocolates and a card, and when I was writing the card to my mother (because she was currently giving me the silent treatment and wasn't talking to me) I realized I didn't know what I was even sorry for, I just knew I had to apologize and let her think that she was right, so she would start talking to me again. But as an adult, this stance in life didn't serve my new relationships at all. It's just no good to have our four-year-old self driving the bus.

Stephen Wolinsky in his book *The Dark Side of The Inner Child* says that the inner-child identity or false self is a time-frozen position that filters reality through a limited distorted lens. The wounded inner child is stuck in time, it needs to be freed from childhood survival mechanisms that no longer fit present-time relationships.

The psychological reality of who we are, as current teachers like Sam Harris and James Fadiman have clarified, is that there is no single self inside anyone. In each situation we find ourselves in, the interaction of our past experiences and the present situation act together to generate our current sense of self. We mentioned this before – how we have many different selves, grounded in the past but responsive in the present. And this doesn't mean we're a split personality or have a personality disorder. It means we're being honest with ourselves, able to accept the fluidity of our identity, and stop grasping onto a fixed identity. We're vastly more than the defensive identity we took on as children.

I often talk with my clients about how all children are in essence powerless. We go from total immersion in our mother's womb into needing caregivers for our every need –

and then we steadily advance into adolescence and puberty, and then that leap into adulthood where we must learn to claim our own power. In John Lee's book *Growing Yourself Back Up*, he says that adults, unlike children, have multiple choices in every situation. Within reason we can choose what we want to buy, who we want to relate with, what work we prefer – but when we were three or four we couldn't look around us and say, "Well my dad's a drunk and my mom is depressed. This house isn't safe for me, so I think I'll leave and go get my own apartment."

Eric Bernie in his book *Games People Play* talks about how, like in a play or movie, there's a set script someone has written that the director and actors must keep acting out over and over again. Our parents have a script for how they want our lives to turn out. And as children we develop a similar script, and then as adults keep trying to act out that pre-determined storyline.

But we're also the producers of our adult lives – we have adult power, and that means we can shut down the script and play we're in charge of (our own lives) and write a new script that suits us much better. We can change our own role, and we can choose new characters to play in our adult life drama. When we seek employment, we can look for a new stage where we can act quite differently than earlier in our lives. If we have been caught up from childhood in an expression of our personality that's overly defensive, anxious, manipulatory or whatever, we can consciously re-introduce ourselves beyond that childhood contortion and find ourselves acting in a play we really like.

I remember a client who spoke about his Aloof Mother. He was a very good-looking man, and one time he told me he went to a party and noticed three women gathered together. Two of them smiled over at him but the other woman didn't. He told me he made a bee line for the one that didn't smile – he was intrigued by her aloofness because it was familiar. He had spent all his childhood trying vainly to gain his mother's attention and approval. And still he was reflexively seeking that approval from every new female relationship he entered into. Finally in therapy he was seeing this pattern, and developing his ability to break out of the pattern into something new.

Psychologists tell us that our pattern of attachment is formed mostly from the age of 6 months to 3 years. This is a very crucial time for developing fundamental expectations about how we bond with other people. At that age we have minimal language abilities and mobility, so we can't do much to control our destiny. We are literally at the mercy of whoever is looking after us. And this early experience forms a bedrock of assumptions which we carry into all our new relationships.

We all leave our family of origin with emotional baggage. We meet someone new, and unconsciously we ask ourselves – will I get rejected? Can I trust this person? Will they meet my deeper needs? Will they abandon me? Will I be dominated and lose my freedom? These questions don't pop out of the blue. They're based on those first years of our lives. And unfortunately our apprehensions from childhood can strongly color how we relate with a new person – and perhaps fatally mess up that relationship.

If history repeats itself and
the unexpected always happens
how incapable must man be
of learning from experience ...

George Bernard Shaw

History repeats itself until we learn the lessons that we need in order to change our path. History repeats itself, as we've seen, mostly because nobody listens and learns. Unaware people go on repeating their past again and again, and therefore cannot bring any newness into their lives. People who live such mechanical lives are easy to predict if we know their past. And usually their lives will feel unfulfilled, empty, emotionally conflicted and spiritually devoid of inspiration.

But of course we tend to stick to what's comfortable, to what we know – rather than be brave and venture into a new way of living, even if it's liberating and revelatory. Marianne Williamson summed this up quite succinctly:

It takes courage to endure
the sharp pains of self-discovery
rather than choose to take
the dull pain of unconsciousness
that would last the rest of our lives

Marianne Williamson

Every time a new client walks into my office, I feel proud of them for just showing up, for risking who knows what in order to break free emotionally and breathe more freely into an expanding sense of who they are. As children we don't really know if our parents are toxic or healthy. Youngsters must breathe the emotional air in their home without judgment, even if from an outside perspective they're being maltreated. Only with the perspective of adulthood can we look back and evaluate our childhood lives.

In her book *Thou Shalt Not Be Aware,* Alice Miller speaks about a client who had been a prostitute who finally could remember how her father would put her on his lap and on occasion masturbate, using her body for his sexual needs. This woman's later life as a prostitute was actually a compulsively repeated re-enactment of the trauma of her early childhood. As a prostitute she offered herself as a plaything to the male like she had as a child – but now as an adult she was able to remain in control over what happened. Unfortunately she still wasn't managing to resolve the wounds of her childhood violation. Only through counseling was she able to see her patterns clearly – and then choose to put them aside in favor of a more healthy, fulfilling and self-affirming life.

An End To Sleepwalking

Many mystics, psychologists and philosophers have told us over the ages that we are 'sleep walking' through our lives as if in a trance. No matter what happens, so many of us resist any kind of fundamental change. Out of fear we prefer the numbing security of our ingrained routines, beliefs, prejudices and assumptions. However difficult or unhappy our lives might be, rather than face the insecurity of discovering something unknown and different, we opt for the familiar patterns we're used to.

As we saw earlier, one of the strongest instincts in human beings is the need to stay immersed in the familiar. There's of course nothing wrong with living a simple life without much change, or being attracted to adult partners who have the same traits as one of our parents. Routine plays an important part in any life. If our new partner is similar to us, we can harmonize quite readily. Difficulties only emerge, as we've been exploring, when we choose a new life partner who has the same negative relationship patterns as a parent with whom we had difficulty.

When we find this type of romantic partner we might feel we are home-free, we've finally teamed up with someone with whom we can resume where we left off with our parent – and finally get things right at last. Perhaps we are attracted to a person as emotionally unavailable as our father, or as controlling as our mother – and now we can heal and evolve that early relationship so that we get what we needed from our parent. This is all of course unconscious and defies logic, but there's great power in an unmet childhood need that is brooding unresolved in the unconscious part of the mind. This adult experiment is usually doomed to failure and heartbreak but it keeps on repeating itself.

Over and over I've seen how the seeds of marital conflict are sown in childhood neglect, insensitivity, absence, anger and abuse. An unconscious purpose of many marriages and other relationships is to heal childhood wounds that beg attention and resolution. The unmet hunger for love, acceptance, safety and trust results a universally-present wound. All parents to one extent or another don't fully meet the deep emotional needs of their children, we're all needing to deal with this core issue as adults.

In this light I would venture to say that almost all adult heartbreaks are childhood heartbreaks playing on repeat-mode. Such is life. And as adults we can either see ourselves as hapless victims – or we can turn childhood suffering into adult growth and liberation. Our bad luck in childhood optimally can become the stimulus for transformation. But first we must break out of our trance, stop sleep-walking through our lives, and start risking whatever it takes to wake up, discover our true selves and purpose – and shift from cocoon to butterfly.

CONCLUSION

Just suppose that you actually picked your family and made a contract with them for this lifetime. They are your curriculum for this lifetime. What challenges and lessons are you called to overcome? What did you need from your family that you did not get? What gift have you come to give your family? Therapeutic Coaching is a unique and innovative method that I use with clients. It is a blend of Psychotherapeutic approaches in addition to Coaching. The focus in Psychotherapy is more on healing from the past, while the focus on Coaching is more on getting you to where you wish to be next. Coaching tends to be goal and action oriented and provides accountability and motivation to clients. I find blending the two approaches works very well.

CHAPTER FOUR

Our Inner Guidance System

~~~~~~~~~~~~~~~~~~~~~~~~~~~~~~

The best thing I have ever learned in my life was learning to tune into my feelings – and to listen to the message that my feelings are trying to communicate to me. I have also learned that a feeling can never be wrong – they're speaking the truth of the moment. And I learned to start listening and validating my feelings – to listen to my gut instincts. We feel what we feel for a reason. And – we cannot heal what we refuse to feel.

I step by step began to understand how to use my feelings as a guide to living a more fulfilling life – and then I learned as a life coach how to help others do the same. Every feeling has intelligence, every feeling contains a hidden message. So even now I encourage you to observe what happens when you stay with a feeling rather than ignoring or rejecting or trying to change it – your fear, your sadness, your doubt, your grief, your heartbreak. Don't try to get rid of it in any way. Just begin to notice without judgment or reaction what you are feeling right now ...

For many people it may be difficult to allow or tolerate or even admit to certain feelings. We're often afraid that our feelings will overwhelm or even obliterate us if we open up to them. But I say to my clients, go ahead, let your heart break into a million pieces if it wants or needs to. Allow yourself to cry, to scream, to feel vulnerable if vulnerability arises in you. Learn to move toward your feelings rather than moving away from
~~~~~~~~~~~~~~~~~~~~~~~~~~~~~~

them. This is often challenging, but the results that emerge are well worth it.

Here's a key fact: feelings that arise have a natural life span. They can only remain with intensity for a short period of time. Can you feel surprised for an hour? Can you cry in despair for twenty minutes, or laugh with joy for ten? Start watching how your emotions come ... and go. This in itself can be liberating – almost always, even the most intense bad feelings will on their own come and go.

Also – very few if any people die from opening up and experiencing their emotions. On the contrary, when they surrender to an overwhelming feeling, ten minutes later they might be feeling deeply relieved and good. Recent studies have shown that emotional tears contain several hormones that immediately elicit good feelings.

I suspect most of us habitually try to distract ourselves from our feelings by getting involved with social media, emails, video games, shopping – there are so many distractions available. And we may numb our feelings with some type of substance, food, alcohol, drugs, weed, or some other form of self-medication. This may seem to work for a while. Yet the more we try to push feelings away, the more they keep cropping up. And as a rule, uncomfortable rejected feelings will become even more insistent as time goes by.

Feelings come like waves – they rise, peak, diminish and dissipate if not interrupted or interfered with. But if blocked, the pressure pushing the emotion gets buried alive. And buried emotions definitely fester and build up even more pressure to burst forth. And often they burst forth in the most inappropriate ways.

In contrast, if you stick with the feeling without distracting yourself, you make possible a primary healing process. You start to free up and hear the message that the feeling is trying to communicate to you. For instance, feeling sad may indicate you have an unfulfilled need to be seen or heard, valued and supported. Feeling angry may be a message to establish and hold a relationship boundary – or even a sign of violation.

Often people experience the same feeling occurring over and over again in various circumstances. Have you noticed a certain feeling that travels with you wherever you go? Some people have anxiety and apprehension as their constant companion, others feel depressed. Shame can also be a recurring emotion, or abandonment.

You might want to keep a note pad for a couple of weeks, and in each situation you move into, write down the dominant emotion you feel. This can be enlightening. Start to really get to know your dominant emotional style. And also notice if certain situations evoke certain emotions. When things go wrong or you're under stress, is it anxiety, anger, frustration, resentment, hopelessness or some other emotion that kicks into gear inside you in that situation? Feel, pay attention, reflect – and set yourself free.

Begin to notice your underlying emotional personality traits. Who are you really in this regard? Do you see yourself as depressed, as an anxious person, as confused or aggressive emotionally? Don't try to analyze yourself – just be aware in an accepting mode. Seek to see the truth of you as an emotional being. Do you always see the world through the lens of one or two dominant emotions? Your emotional style or fixation might habitually be subjugation, failure, unlovability, perfectionism, vulnerability, anxiety.

Just keep watching – learn to accept who you really are! And in that process, you'll discover that you begin to change for the better. This is what self-discovery is all about ... being mindful of every moment inside your own body.

Outward Flowing Energy

Our emotions come with an energetic charge to them. Often they are a flow of good feelings – love, satisfaction, pleasure. A pressure builds up inside us to express our good feelings, and this feeling comes flowing out. Without this emotional ebb and flow of our feelings, we're nothing more than cold biorobots. In a deep sense, we are how we feel moment to moment. And when we think of someone we know, we usually have an immediate sense in our hearts of that person as an emotional presence. If they're often antagonistic and unfriendly, we feel this energetically in our hearts because we've felt it before in their presence. Conversely we feel a warm emotion when thinking of someone we love.

And of course, sometimes certain feelings aren't at all fun to experience – emotions like shame, anxiety, grief, anger or rejection. But as we're seeing, ignoring them simply doesn't work. You chronically lose out on the important messages they carry. Feeling hungry guides you to eat, feeling tired guides you to sleep. Your feelings inform you of a need that's calling out. Again – the messages your various feelings communicate are vitally important. If you don't listen to them, physically over time they will fester and cause relationship conflict, health problems, social isolation, even spiritual crises and mental illness. Successfully negotiating this emotional dimension of your life is serious business!

But so often the last thing we want to do is tune into and witness our own feelings. Why? Because feelings can hurt! And many of us learned early on in life that feelings aren't safe to express. Seldom do I find parents who are fully open to let their children express their spontaneous feelings. It's considered the job of parents to condition their children through punishment or love-withdrawal to be good little children – and of course some of this disciplining is needed. As we saw earlier, socialization is necessary for kids to learn how to fit into their community.

But there's another approach to parenting – openly and honestly teaching one's children about how to manage and yet not stifle arising emotions. And for ourselves equally – we need to learn how to greet and treat our feelings as friends and guides. Maybe a feeling is arising to guide us toward some kind of action. You need a hug – so you open up to receive a hug. You need to resolve a conflict, so you express that need. You're lonely, so you get up and go out so that you have the opportunity to relate and feel included.

Also you'll find that sometimes it's enough to on your own feel a particular emotion all the way through until it dissipates. Sometimes a feeling just needs to be witnessed and validated by your own self. Feelings that are being chronically repressed are usually ones that we're deep-down afraid of that threaten to violate our normal sense of who we are. Our parents or someone else in authority made us feel ashamed of expressing a feeling, or actually punished us as young children – and then ever after we're afraid to let that feeling rise to the fore and come out into the open.

This same scenario has happened to every two-to-four-year-old, it's part of the human predicament. We all tend to protect ourselves by blocking every raw surge of uncontrolled energy that pushes for open expression. Out of habit we instantly choke down sudden sensations of charged emotion running throughout our body. In essence we fear ever running out of control. Earlier in this book we talked about this theme in a different way – how we develop an ego that tries to control and override our deeper human feelings. We even dissociate our sense of who we are from our gut feelings – we turn them into our enemy rather than honoring and learning from them as our internal coach and guide.

So much time and energy throughout our lives is wasted trying to hold in a feeling, struggling under pressure not to allow emotional energy to flow outward. It's almost a cliché to point out that the Latin word for emotion, *emovere,* means "to move out, to remove". An emotion is a verb – it's an action. Most animals have fairly uncomplicated emotions, but we human beings in our social and linguistic complexity seem to employ emotions in a vast array of meanings.

Still, at heart our feelings are simple. They alert us to the fact that some sort of action is needed in order to relieve an inner need – and our emotions are what push us into this action. We speak of not feeling motivated, or feeling moved to do something. We can feel inspired to get up and act. And we can simply feel moved – by music, by drama, by a work of art. We can feel we're in danger and move away or deal with the danger. We feel loved and we open our hearts. We feel eager and we stand up to participate. We feel tired and we sit or lie down. In a very real energetic biological way, over and over each day we're continually being informed, provoked and led by ... our feelings.

Another key point – emotions are not thoughts. Thoughts can provoke an emotion, and emotions can surely provoke thoughts. But it's important to pay attention often, to look and see which is causing which. A thought can occur in your mind without any experiential dimension – but an emotion must be actually physically experienced. And as with all animals, we move away from pain, physical or emotional. In fact an emotion is always physical. Therefore we reflexively tend to avoid that discomfort or emotional pain.

So once we've been conditioned to avoid our emotions, we must consciously and intentionally decide to allow the discomfort to stay present, so that we allow it to run its course, reveal its message, and then be done. But usually we don't. For instance we feel a deep sense of loss – but rather than allowing ourselves to experience the loss and go into the emptiness and move through it, we try to fill the emptiness with food, drink, sex, work, media or whatever will distract us away from the negative feeling.

So yes, it takes a bit of courage and inner strength to do this emotional healing work. But trust me – this is the only way to transcend congested emotions, to admit, heal and be done with past emotional wounds that still grip you. And you'll discover that as you stay with the negative emotion, as you learn to translate the messages your feelings are trying to tell you, a direct conduit to your own higher wisdom becomes activated.

Merging Head, Heart ... and Gut

It seems that many or even most adults moving through their daily lives pay scant attention to what I consider their most accurate sense of all – their gut feelings. I like to refer to the three brains: the mind, the heart – and the gut. Reason seems to live mostly in the head, love in the heart, and intuition in the belly. Taken together in balance, these three inner centers of the body represent our compass guiding us through life.

If you look back on your childhood, unless you were very lucky with your parents and schooling, you received minimal education regarding how to integrate your three centers mentioned above into a coherent whole. Welcome to the club. No wonder we feel fragmented, pulled in several directions at once when we make decisions.

Some people seem to naturally realize they are more than their thinking heads. But most of us either never resolve this seeming split, or consciously work toward integration. And there's a rank order to how most of us perceive our inner workings. We place primary value on our reasoning heads in our current culture. Then comes our emotional feelings in the heart - and vaguely comes the third primary guiding force in our bodies - our gut instincts, our intuitive hunches, our core emotional base that we feel in our belly.

Take a look yourself. First, focus in your head. Herein reside your visual sensors, your auditory sensors, you smell sensors, your balance sensors. This is indeed your command center in many ways. And so you probably spend most of your awareness time in your head, right? But notice - you don't really feel much emotional charge and release in your head. You take in valuable information about the outside world in your head. You do all your cognitive deductive thinking in your head. Good.

But troubles start when the thinking mind becomes dissociated from the feelings in your heart and gut. Little kids don't have that problem. It's only when we begin to develop our sense of self, our unique identity that we begin to struggle. Our heart and gut might say do one thing - but our mind says hold on, you'll get in trouble if you do that. So out of fear of getting punished or rejected for following our heart and gut, we learn to block those inputs.

This development is mostly unavoidable, even with the best of parents. But we don't have to go through our whole lives dissociated from our heart/belly feelings. This is one of the main jobs of a life coach - to help integrate all three primary functions into an integrated whole. Most clients coming to me don't understand the significance of their feelings. But quite soon they can come to deeply respect, listen to, evaluate and then act on the wisdom of the lower duo.

Several of the body/mind sciences have recently discovered the complex neurological communication system linking gut, heart and head. And in the process, the gut has become seriously linked with what's going on higher up. You can Google this research if you want to learn more – it's important! Being blindly dominated by gut instinct is usually not a good idea – but listening to the message of the gut, and integrating this message into heart-felt impulses and higher reasoning – this is the path I find most effective in developing a better life.

And how is this done? Again – by focusing your power of attention directly toward your heart, and your gut – and developing that inner attention muscle so that you regularly look to your heart and gut to see what's going on there, before making decisions and going into action.

Try this right now. Just become aware of your head, and all the 'thinking buzz' going on as you read these pages. And now shift your focus of awareness to your breathing ... and whatever feelings you might find in your heart right now. And ... just breathe into whatever feelings you discover. Allow that sensory information to become conscious in your thinking mind. Don't judge what you discover – just be aware, accept, and observe how this 'lower information' affects your higher mental processes.

You'll need to move through this process many times before it becomes a new valued habit. At first you'll want to take time – but after a while, wherever you are, you can instantly 'look down' and bring your deeper feelings to mind. Tune into the signals. Trust them. You've been conditioned not to trust your heart or your gut. I'm saying get beyond this conditioning. It takes time to educate your heart and gut to the fact that you now want to trust them, to listen to them. They have been out of the spotlight for so long, it might take them a while to find their own wisdom center. Just persevere. Become whole again!

For instance, you might focus in your gut and find that you feel hungry. Your heart might resonate with this, because yes, you do love to eat goodies. But then you bring this info to your mind and it says – no! Don't listen to your gut, you're on a diet. I'm in charge and you're not going to give in to munching impulses. What to do? Instead of seeing these three centers as fighting each other, begin to see them as a team, working together to make the best decisions. Learn to dialog as a trio – and harmoniously find compromises that suit you.

Where Do Feelings Come From?

A lot of times feelings seem to arise out of the blue – we suddenly find ourselves caught up in a reactive emotion but we don't really know where it came from. This happens because we're just not focused at all upon our emotional senses until they become acute and demand attention. If we habitually feel sad or depressed, anxious or aggressive, we don't register these feelings hardly at all. We can't identify those feelings, let alone express them. Sadly, it's been documented that when under stress, our EQ goes out the window.

Studies show that at least in our Western society, a third of the population reports being habitually anxious, and another third habitually depressed. Feeling such pervasive emotions as a habit means the person is continually under pressure emotionally. That's why some people react with explosive feelings with slight provocation – the pressure is just waiting for an excuse to release.

A fair share of my coaching clients come to me because they're expressing inappropriate emotions that are causing problems in their lives and they don't know what to do about controlling them. My response is two-fold. First, begin to accept and honor the feelings. Then look to see where the original source of the anxiety or depression or whatever came from. Then learn to listen to that feeling each time it appears, and step by step defuse the explosions.

While doing all this, something wonderful happens – the negative emotion becomes a positive guide. There's a time and place to feel anxious – and to do something about the situation causing the anxiety. And yes, there are times when depression is appropriate if we don't get stuck in it. Life can feel hopeless at times – we lose our job, a friend deserts us, someone we love dies. Feeling depressed is then both expected and also a push to do something to move beyond the suffering.

But rather than using negative emotions to push us forward into better feelings, we're surrounded by big-pharma's multibillion-dollar industry pushing magical pills promising chemical relief from emotional suffering. But these pills only suppress feelings and emotions – which makes recovery and self-discovery ever harder if not impossible. Especially with clients using anti-depressants or anti-anxiety medications, when I ask them about their feelings they give me an answer on how they think. Their mind refuses to consider and reveal their actual feelings.

We seem to live under the false notion that if we don't look at bad feelings they will go away. We have been taught to deny, bypass, endure, escape, run away from our negative feelings. Instead we try to go numb inside. But unfortunately, we can't heal what we don't feel. All our feelings want is to be attended to. When we deny a particular emotion, we're denying a part of ourselves. Something happened in our past that messed up our emotions – and only with the power of loving attention can we accept all of our past, release the original emotional memory, and genuinely recover.

I have learned to let each of my feelings make themselves known as they arise, and as the feeling comes up I say: "I see you, I feel you, I hear you – and I accept you." Feelings, as you'll discover, want to be heard lovingly, without judgment, without criticism, and without advice. As a coach I listen a lot – and usually I don't have to say much. The process of listening in and of itself generates the desired healing. It's the same with listening to your own feelings. You're not listening to solve anything. You're just letting your feelings have their say so that they don't have to torture you to evoke attention. Again – our emotions when flowing freely give us deep wise inputs if we listen.

Where Do Your Emotions Live?

In so many ways, you are your body. You might hold vast concepts in your thinking conceptual mind about your body – but with feelings, that doesn't matter. What matters is recognizing that a feeling is under pressure to communicate with you – and also noticing where in your physical body you're feeling this emotion. Where does this emotion reside? Often an unrecognized emotional tension, building over time, will generate definite physical pain such as a back ache, head ache, pain in the stomach or chest, and so forth. But often a more subtle emotional pain will be free-floating, or not seeming to be related with a particular function of the body.

Consider your own body right now. Would you say you're feeling good or bad in your body? And where do you feel this most intensely? Also, is this a recurring pain in that location?

And ... what happens if you just pause and breathe into this location in your body – how does the pain change in intensity?

It's important to notice that unless you have definite physical injury, your awareness of a pain spot in your body changes fairly rapidly. If you have an itch and don't scratch it but just watch it, you'll find that the itch goes away rather quickly. This is important – pain changes as your attention watches without reacting.

Try it for yourself. Discover that pain is a variable – and you can influence your level of sensitivity by holding attention to an irritant without trying to change it – it will change on its own! There's a whole new science exploring long-term pain where there's no actual physical cause. Instead, the nervous system become hyper-sensitive and provokes the sensation of pain. Look deeply at this experience as it happens, and you'll find that attention itself generates healing. And this goes for all emotions, good and bad. Healing energy flows where attention goes.

Like many people, I tend to feel a lot of emotion in my solar plexus. But different emotions can be located in different regions of the body. Where do you tend to feel love? And how about anger? Where do you feel sadness? Joy? Confusion? Hunger? Sexual attraction? Begin to pause regularly, ask yourself what emotion you're primarily feeling – and look to see where you're feeling this emotion. That's a primary 'do it often' process in self-discovery.

Emotions – Past And Present

A good question to ask when an intense feeling comes up is: "When in the past have I felt exactly this same way?" This question can be highly insightful, leading you to discover the origins of the feeling. When an intense emotion comes up and grabs at you, it's usually not just in reaction to your current situation. One of your emotional buttons is getting pushed. See if you can pause right in the middle of the reaction – and look to see what memories might spring to mind. Try to recall other times when you have had the same feeling. Go right into the heart of the feeling, and discover what is at the core.

Usually you'll find that there's some particular person in your past associated with the emotion you're feeling in the present. As we discussed earlier, we often attract people into our lives who enable us to feel whatever we've repressed, so that we can bring the original traumatic experience up in our memory, feel the original reaction we had, and open to healing and letting go of the memory. To feel it is to heal it – and we continue to be run by whatever we don't heal. Life is actually giving you a hand by presenting you with people who evoke unpleasant feelings buried within. Your challenge is to bring those early emotions up into conscious awareness.

I remember once when I was co-facilitating a program that I had designed, and the other facilitator was being quite bossy, telling me what to do. As she took over preparations that I had already put in place, I could feel anger and then rage bubbling up inside me. I felt very constricted around my solar plexus. I sat with the feelings she was triggering in me – and found myself realizing that her energy reminded me of my mother who was very controlling, her motto was "my way or the highway." Thank god I had the awareness to see that this facilitator was just the catalyst. I stayed with the present anger until it dissipated. There was no need to confront the facilitator. She seemed to be the cause – but actually she was the catalyst for me to get in touch with and let go of old pain from my past.

Just always remember that it's the inner child who gets its buttons pushed, not the adult. Feelings come from within us.

People can bring up a painful past occurrence only if it's already in our mind. Except for an obvious present-moment violation, someone in the present can trigger anger in us if there's already past anger already hidden under pressure inside us. I know this seems obvious but so often people are unaware of the whole process.

When someone triggers you, if you are honest and in touch with yourself you can own the upset and throw no blame. You can say "Aha – this is a great opportunity to see something inside of myself that needs to be witnessed, accepted, looked at and released." People might trigger my fear, for instance – but not cause it. Understanding this dynamic can eliminate loads of present-moment conflict.

React Or Respond?

When talking about feelings we always need to understand and deal with the universal human process of emotional regression. Emotional regression is when something happens in our present-moment experience and triggers a memory and related emotion in our mind and body. Right at that moment, if we're being mindful, we have the choice of either reacting or responding to the trigger. Much of life depends on which choice we make.

Actually when we react there's no reflective thought involved at all. The stimulus hits us – and we automatically react with predetermined emotions and actions. If we allow zero time between the stimulus and the response, if we react, we're not really conscious at that moment at all. We're acting as a biorobot that lacks the reflective power to take in a stimulus and ... not instantly react.

Instead, humans have the unique power to experience a stimulus that provokes an old reaction – and if even for a few seconds, reflect on what's happening inside us. We can catch our auto-play reaction, our reflexive regression into a past defensive emotional programming – and perhaps choose not to react. Instead we can quickly reflect on our present situation, and choose to respond appropriately in that present situation.

If a stimulus instantly (and often quite unconsciously) wakes up a memory of some old situation that provoked a negative (and usually defensive) emotion and perhaps behavior, this regression into the past can provoke an over-reaction, or perhaps an under-reaction. We can lash out at someone, or we can freeze in inaction – with neither alternative being appropriate in the present circumstance.

Maybe our boss calls us into their office – and all of a sudden we're no longer a grown and capable person. We instantly regress back to feeling like a four-year-old kid whose mother has just said threateningly "wait till your father gets home!" Or perhaps your teacher once sent you off to the principal for punishment. Your boss calling you into their office pushes this fear-based memory button, it wakes up the apprehension of imminent punishment – and even though you're an adult who does good work, your whole body is suddenly tingling with fear, you're sweating and feel weak, you can hardly catch your breath.

And so you walk into your boss' office defensive, muddled in your mind, and perhaps react in ways that damage your adult position. But you do have the choice, if you can remember and act on it, to pause just for a few breaths, reflect on what's happening inside you – and snap out of the regressive reaction. You might need to practice this reflection-response process for a while (and that's part of what a coach will do with you) but you no longer need to be a victim of your own regressive patterns. Between the stimulus and the response you can transform your life.

Many of us regress when even strangers do very simple things that remind us of the past. Someone butts into line ahead of you and you find yourself suddenly consumed in anger at that person. If you freeze that reaction, you're stuck with bottled-up hostility that will spill out into future engagements. If you release your regressive anger you might find yourself in a verbal or even physical fight that benefits no one.

Usually regressive behavior is an expression of having once felt seriously violated as a child. You had to bottle this feeling instead of releasing it back then – but ever after (unless you do something about it) you'll keep on irrationally reacting in similar situations. Feeling violated as a child can seem like a life-or-death experience. Kids naturally react to unfairness, punishment, judgment and bullying because their emerging sense of self is being threatened. Their whole world can suddenly feel like it's been shattered when their physical or emotional integrity is being violated – and therefore their adult regression can be quite explosive.

From a coaching perspective I like to think that when regressing, we are unconsciously using a present situation to expose lingering issues from the past that need observation and healing. Losing control for instance, or feeling absolutely devastated when a friend rejects us, might well be a clue that we have regressed – and that we need to pause and recognize this. If we're feeling hotly upset with anyone, good questions to ask ourselves are: "What's going on here – when did I feel like this before? Who does this person remind me of from my past? And how can I right now change this reactive pattern?"

Most of our adult heartbreaks definitely go back to childhood heartbreaks, and our adult failures so often are rooted in childhood failures. And even very small present situations can evoke an over-strong reaction. Whenever we feel a heightened charge in our body, more than the present circumstance warrants, we need to pause and ask ourselves if we're regressing back to some earlier experience.

And here's something really wonderful about the general process of emotional healing. Awareness itself is the healer. The simple process of nonjudgmentally witnessing an interior reaction, and seeing clearly its origin, can elicit deep healing – because you're finally admitting to something that hurt you in the past (violation, shame, etc.) ... and by seeing that you in fact survived that hurt, as an adult you can therefore let it all go and be done with it.

And in this process we can see another deep truth. We tend to think our unhappiness comes from some external event or person or situation. We are taught to look outside for the cause of our feelings rather than to look within. In essence we lay blame outward rather than putting all blame aside and looking within for a solution to our unhappiness. If you look at yourself in this regard, you'll probably realize that as Shakespeare said, "There's nothing right or wrong, but thinking makes it so." If we are constantly telling ourselves that the outside world is making us unhappy or anxious or depressed, our down-thoughts will color the outside world with this assumption. Again, we're ultimately creating our world through the thoughts we think. Said another way, we're hurting ourselves through the attitudes we maintain.

Three Phases Of An Emotion

Let's look a bit closer at how emotions are created and emerge. There are usually three levels in expressing our feelings. The first level is physiological. We find our bodies feeling in a particular way, with an emotional charge. This feeling is provoked, as we just saw, by something happening from outside our body, or from a memory or thought happening inside us. Each basic emotion has its own physiological signature – we might shake with anger or rage, we might shiver and contract in fear, we might go limp and collapse in depression, cringe with guilt, and so forth. In a reactive emotion we instantly act out our preprogrammed expression of this emotion without any reflection at all. As mature adults we observe and acknowledge how we're currently feeling, learn from the observation – and respond appropriately to the present situation.

The second level of an emerging emotion, if we've learned self-reflection, is to put into words a simple statement of how and what we're feeling. Emotions live in quite different regions of the brain than does our reasoning function – so verbalizing how we feel serves to welcome our 'higher mental function' into the process. "Ah, I'm suddenly feeling hostile toward Sam for no reason," you might say to yourself. And this first thought will lead (especially if you're working on this process) to old memories and new insights. The key of this second phase is to stay tuned into your feelings while you think about them.

The third part of emotional expression is of course physical release of the internal feelings. Thinking about a feeling isn't enough – you must also allow for the release of that emotion. If you've acknowledged and reflected on what you're feeling, you'll usually still benefit from encouraging that feeling to come flowing out and thus be expressed and gone. Otherwise you'll still be stuck with the emotional pressure, and might also stay caught up in over-thinking the emotional situation.

Something made you feel sad or depressed – let the tears flow. If you're alone, you can perhaps shout out loud to release the emotion. If you're angry, go ahead and perhaps bash a pillow. Let yourself tremble if anxiety is gripping you, or do any other physical expression that's suitable. This is a level of expression that a coach can help greatly with, so that you feel safe and accepted for going deeply into the feeling.

With this physical expression, you're in fact regressing, but in a safe healing manner. You had this expressive capacity as a child, you could express your feelings quite spontaneously. Little kids cry easily, they have a temper tantrum, they get angry with a playmate for taking their toy. They also express joy and love, contentment and awe. They release the feeling and then ten minutes later they're feeling some other feeling.

But as we grew up, as noted before, we learned to control our feelings – and in most cases we unfortunately learned to over-control so that we'd avoid punishment or guilt. Thus we became less and less aware of our inner feelings, and buried our natural emotional-release process. In my opinion, most of us really need to relearn as adults how to effectively and positively share our inner feelings with the world around us. We're in essence, if we admit it, in need of remedial classes on emotional release and healing.

This goes for the positive emotions as well as the negative ones. In fact each emotion is of equal value in or lives – otherwise evolutionary-wise we wouldn't have all the emotions we do. Becoming able to fully express love and joy and hope as adults is equally important as relearning how to express and release and heal anxiety and hopelessness and so forth.

Like I said, relearning to tune into and then express and release our feelings can take time – but it's time worth taking. Our emotional feelings are probably the biggest part of what makes us human. We live so much in our heads, in thoughts about the past and the future, in plans and regrets and so forth, that we ignore what we're feeling in our bodies in the present moment – but really, take away our feelings, and what's the point of life? If we want to avoid the pain of emotions and therefore try to hide, ignore, repress and deny our feelings, we are in essence committing emotional suicide. We actually don't ever escape our buried emotional pain – but sadly we do lose the emotional pleasures of life.

The Language Of Feeling

There's such a price to pay for maintaining our inability to deal in healthy ways with our feelings. And certain languages can express emotions better than others. It's correctly said that Spanish is the loving tongue for instance, as they have many subtle words and meanings to express the complex variations in romantic love.

English is not really very good in talking about feelings of love. And unfortunately, long-gone origins of ingrained emotional constriction can run in families for many generations. You might want to look back at your own emotional inheritance in this regard – did your parents pick up emotional constriction from their parents, and did those parents from their parents? Could your parents express their emotions clearly and openly, or was there loads of taboo topics they never spoke to you about because they also inherited those constrictions?

Growing up in my Drogheda family, the language of feelings was quite alien to me. My parents couldn't handle their emotional lives, which gave my siblings and I no chance of handling ours. I remember when my father went into the Rutland Centre for treatment for his alcoholism, every second Sunday we had to attend a family day. I was about 14 years of age at the time, and during one of those meetings the Counsellor asked me how was I feeling?

I looked over at my sister and the two of us suddenly broke into a fit of laughing. I realize now that the laughter was nervousness – I hadn't a clue how I was feeling, and I definitely had no way to put into words how I was feeling. This was like learning a new language to me. My mother was then asked how she felt, and I could see that my mom was so uncomfortable with the question that she said she needed to use the bathroom.

That evening driving home in the car, my mother told us that we would not be going to those meetings again. I could see that the language of feelings was totally alien to our family. I became numb and disassociated from my feelings, so naturally I couldn't even think, let along talk about them. Only when I left home did I begin to search for help with opening up.

Feelings are a form of information. This means that when we are not in tune with our feelings we are continually missing vital information. In our family we had a long sad history of disregarding our feelings. I remember that if I cried I was told by one of my parents that they'd really give me something to cry about. If I was laughing and my mother didn't see the funny side of things, I was told she'd put that smile the other side of my face. If I expressed anger I was told don't talk to me in that tone young lady. So my feelings were dismissed all the time.

What about you and your childhood emotional freedom? I'm not asking you to judge and blame or accuse your parents and caregivers. Everyone does their best, depending on their own upbringing and their ability to take responsibility for their emotional expressions. But it's important to look back and recognize the emotional atmosphere you grew up in, from loving to sorta okay to toxic.

When you cried as a kid, how did your parents respond? When you got mad, same thing – what was their reaction? When you were sad, did they allow you to have your feelings, or try to make you snap out of it? Take some time over the next days to reflect deeply on this issue. Perhaps make notes, be nonjudgmental, honest and thorough. This is a definite path to self-discovery.

Also, see if you can remember times when emotions were discussed. What words were used, and what attitudes were presented toward those words. Did people say to you, "Don't cry like a sissy"? Did showing emotions in general get treated as a weakness? Were you judged when you felt frightened? Were you punished when reacting out loud with anger to a perceived violation of your person and space? Take time to reflect, to accept, to heal and let go.

Emotional Intelligence

Let's get one thing clear: nobody is born with emotional intelligence. It's clearly an acquired skill. As kids we learned from felt experience and adult teaching how to manage, modify, respect and value our emotional selves. And notice this – mindfulness at any age is required in order to gain emotional intelligence. We must be able to observe and recognize our own feelings, and also those of other people. If we're lucky we grew up with emotionally-wise role models, and we simply imprinted on their daily emotional resonance and behavior. If not so lucky, we just did our best to survive emotionally, and step by step come to understand who we are as emotional bodies and beings.

Take anxiety for example. Anxiety is a signal that we feel something is beyond our control, usually something in our lurking future that threatens us. Everyone develops some form of worrying about the future. We might feel our anxiety as a queasy ache in our solar plexus. Often anxiety is a wholebody weakness, tension or apprehension. In our early years we won't even have a name for it – but at some point we'll learn that we're feeling something called anxiety. It's said that "when you name it you tame it."

Everyone early on learns that they can feel happy or unhappy, funny or sad, afraid or angry – but for each of us, the related feelings in our body will be different, unique. This is a deep part of developing our sense of who we are, our unique identity, our self-awareness. And for a great many people, if they're honest, they'll answer the question of "What kind of person are you?" with "I'm an unhappy person, I'm a sad person, I'm a depressed or anxious person." They might glibly and defensively first react with the superficial words "I'm a happy person." But dig down just a bit and, as studies document, you'll discover that so many people are identified with a negative emotion. And if you find that you are – then hey – decide to change that for the better!

When clients struggle to express and label how they feel, I often give them a chart with a range of 'feeling vocabulary' and get them to familiarize themselves with this new language. Then I discuss with them when and where it's appropriate to express these feelings, depending on the situation, whether it's personal, a work setting or a larger context. Once they've learned to identify a feeling and put a name on it, they can learn skills to regulate their feelings rather than acting them out inappropriately or burying them.

Feelings definitely motivate us into action, either to approach someone, to avoid something, or to 'play dead' and avoid a confrontation. These are common mammalian emotions – the universal fight, flight or freeze response. And each of us has personality-markers related to this triad of responses. I get clients to become familiar with their particular response style. Is their style to fight, is it to run away – or is it to clam up and freeze? And what about you?

Note that the 'fight' reaction is associated with aggression and anger. The 'run away' reaction is associated with anxiety. The 'play dead' reaction is usually associated with depression and hopelessness. We tend to get tough and attack, get scared and run away, or get depressed and play dead. Do note that in nature, these three reactions to danger are important and effective, not bad at all. It's only with humans, where we repress these natural defense mechanisms, that we get into long-term emotional trouble.

In the program I brought to women in domestic-abusive relationships I also spoke about shame. It's so important in emotional intelligence, and yet not discussed often enough. There are numerous studies on the relationship between shame and violence. When a child grows up feeling shamed, humiliated or ridiculed, too often this chronic put-down 'loss of face' experience ends up turning into random acts of aggression and violence.

Prison inmates often say that when asked why they had assaulted someone, it was because "he dissed me" – meaning someone disrespected or shamed them. A lot of violent people carry a guarded secret about being shamed as a child. And they end up feeling ashamed even to reveal what shames them.

Take a moment and think about something in your life that you are terrified of anyone finding out about. Do you have a shameful experience in your past where even the thought of this being exposed mortifies you? Did you do (or not do) something that even now causes you to want to curl up in a ball, pull a blanket over your head and hide from the world? A shamed person would dearly like to become completely invisible – thus the old saying: "I wanted the ground to open up and swallow me."

But like all unaccepted emotions, burying shame is what gives it power over you. Shame thrives in darkness and decreases when we shine the light of awareness on it. So bring your feelings of shame into the open – talk about them. Shame is all about being judged for having done something wrong – but who are you letting decide what's right or wrong? And if you still judge yourself for something you did, then it's time to learn how to accept yourself just as you are ... and to forgive yourself for past deeds.

CHAPTER FIVE

Your Feelings Won't Kill You

~~~~~~~~~~~~~~~~~~~~~~~~~~~~~~~~

I remember a client telling me she felt that if she started crying that she might never stop. And many clients unconsciously seem to actually fear that if they gave in to their feelings, they wouldn't survive the onslaught – their high charge of negative repressed feelings would consume them. Of course the reality is just the opposite. Releasing pent-up emotions almost always feels better afterwards. Therefore I assure my clients that their feelings won't kill them.

I also assure them that feelings have a natural time span. Allowing expression of one's true feelings frees up energy that was previously spent pushing buried feelings down. The more we allow our authentic feelings to be felt, the more energy and attention we have to devote to our everyday lives.

An outflowing emotion does have a natural life span. It can only remain with intensity for a short time. Have you ever cried for more than fifteen minutes at a time, or laughed, or stayed angry? Overt emotional expression comes and is done. It's only the repressed emotions such as depression (which is usually repressed anger) and anxiety (which is usually repressed fright) and shame (which is usually repressed self-judgment) that can literally live a lifetime pent up inside.

Although there are obviously illnesses that are physiological in origin, many psychologists now say that a large percentage of diseases are caused by chronically repressed and denied emotions. As the saying goes, you can't heal what you won't feel. It's so unfortunate that earlier generations were never
~~~~~~~~~~~~~~~~~~~~~~~~~~~~~~~~

taught emotional intelligence in school – and even now this is just beginning to happen.

I feel that a primary role of a life coach is to hopefully accelerate the expansion of emotional intelligence in our culture. As mentioned earlier, emotional intelligence is the ability to understand, interpret and respond to your feelings in a healthy appropriate way. People with healthy emotional intelligence are able to process and express their authentic feelings quite naturally. But without the ability to understand our feelings we can become lost and sometimes seriously stuck. Expressing our feelings won't kill us – but repressing them can ultimately lead to disease and even death.

Take anger for example. Our anger is not intended to be projected onto someone else. It is more a wake-up call alerting us to change something within our lives that is threatening. It's important not to be afraid of anger. Instead we can use its energetic charge to push us toward identifying what's threatening us – and then make changes and reduce the identified danger. Rather than blaming some outside person and aiming your aggression toward that person, you can use the anger to propel change in your life. Then the anger will be gone.

We also never need to be embarrassed for needing to cry. Crying at appropriate times is a sign of courage. It's a sign that you can be real and authentic and show your vulnerability, which is actually a strength. Too many people, especially men, feel ashamed when they express their feelings as tears. In the American west the cliché was (and still is among macho males) that 'cowboys don't cry'. I feel sorry for the cowboys and all the current 'tough-guy' cultural variations on that macho theme. And of course women have been caught in this tearless void as well, and shamed when they shed authentic tears.

Overall, I think it's accurate to say that in our over-busy society we are not allowed much space at all for our feelings. When someone close to us dies and we're trying to move through grieving and come to terms with this huge loss, and society affords us a scant few days of grieving – then we're expected to just keep going as usual to work and so forth as if nothing had happened. And of course we can bury our emotional pain by staying submerged in the swamp of non-stop social media.

No wonder most of us have so much unprocessed emotional pressure. No wonder we stay obsessed with past traumatic experiences. We're not being given the opportunity to work through the terrible feelings we had at the time. We have no cultural space to work through how we were impacted by the trauma. Instead we were taught to put on a brave face and get on with life. I see clients all the time grieving for what their younger selves went through years ago.

For instance there's almost nothing more traumatizing than a romantic breakup where you feel your heart was literally broken. But for most people, there's minimal help in recovering from such a trauma – and it just festers inside, sometimes literally for the rest of a person's life. The following succinct quote expresses this:

I never get angry, I grow a tumor instead.

Woody Allen

This might strike us as funny – but then we quickly realize that it's actually tragic. I don't mean to imply that everyone who's sick needs to go through an intense emotional-release process – but this dimension definitely needs consideration.

Bits Of Frozen History

There is almost no disease,
mental or physical, without repression.

Dr Arthur Janov

In his book *The New Primal Scream,* Arthur Janov talks about how early traumatic experience becomes imprinted in our minds where it continues to subliminally torture us: "There are two ways in which imprints are set in place. One is through the experience of a single excruciating drama, the other is through a series of events during which certain needs remain chronically unfulfilled over a period of several years."

Negative emotional imprints are basically bits of frozen history. Young children naturally imprint on many things in their environment, mostly the behaviors they observe in their parents. This is a primary built-in system for rapidly and deeply learning how to function as a human being in society. But when an experience traumatizes the child, the experience freezes in memory and remains unexpressed and unresolved.

This is the classic PTSD wound – and most young children unavoidably are exposed to a great many such traumas that their parents and caregivers don't even know happened. Some seemingly insignificant experience, for instance the parents fighting and shouting momentarily at each other, can imprint into a young child's memory and remain a sticking point long into adulthood. That's just how life goes.

I'd say that most repressed emotions and PTSD contractions are ultimately rooted in a child's unmet needs. A child needs to feel safe and secure – but with parents regularly arguing and even fighting, the child's need for security is being continually damaged. And certainly at school, emotional trauma is a recurrent experience. Kids can be so mean to each other! And so we emerge as adults with a whole pack of repressed feelings and trauma experiences – and as we move through our stressful adult lives, no wonder our bodies often start to break down with various trauma-related symptoms.

If the big killer in the world today is repression, it's also true that there is nothing more healing, and more preventive of disease, than liberated free-flowing feelings. If you mis-learned the healthy dynamic of loving and being loved, for instance, then as an adult you're going to need to identify your misunderstanding of how to love – and break free from your initial false imprint. If you initially learned to repress your natural expression of all your full range of human emotions, as an adult you're going to need to treat yourself as an emotional remedial learner and discover who you really are as a liberated emotional being.

Curiously, when an adult finally gets in touch with their real emotional needs, and realizes they've been numb to their emotions their whole lives, there is often an overwhelming sense of sadness, of regret for all the energy and time wasted in struggling ineffectively to get their inner needs met. So many people struggle for instance to gain the unconditional love they hungered for as children. They go from one relationship to the next seeking someone who will give them what their mother failed to – and of course this is an impossible search, for as adults we must give ourselves this unconditional love, not expect other people to give it to us.

Bethany Webster in her book *Discovering The Inner Mother* named this process 'Giving Up the Impossible Dream'. The impossible dream is that one day if we just look hard enough or change ourselves enough, our current mother-figure will finally satisfy our childhood need. Life coaching must often deliver the blow that searching for the perfect relationship will always be futile. As long as a person clings to any false hope, there's no opportunity for insight and healing to happen – so yes, sometimes sadness for the loss of a false dream must be a part of the adult healing process.

The impossible dream is a coping mechanism in which a child hopes that one day when she becomes 'good enough' her mother will finally recognize her and give her the love that she has always longed for. It gives the child a powerful form of hope and a sense of control over her environment. The impossible dream is in fact a brilliant survival strategy for getting through some form of trauma. It takes the focus off the mother and puts the focus on the child, on a future time when all will be well.

When a child feels rejected or judged or dismissed, unconsciously that child believes "there must be something wrong with me." And the child's control of the situation lies in changing themselves into what the parent wants the child to be – but of course it's a false hope and at some point must be let go of, for true recovery to happen. Giving up the impossible dream means realizing the fact that one's parent's pain and judgment had nothing to do with the child.

A child needs to feel accepted for what she is – and if she is not, then to survive in the family she is forced to become phony, to repress her true feelings, to act like she's someone else. And this is total disaster. We all need to be able to be ourselves and be natural. We all need to be comfortable in our own skin. But a lot of the time, as children we cannot be what we are and feel what we feel. *LET ME BE* is the frequent inner cry from deep down in a child's heart. Bu too often, no one hears the cry.

As we're seeing, most of us have a gigantic amount of repressed pain compressed in our bodies that we are usually not even aware of. We just go numb. We become dissociated from the real us. And this prison can seem a lifetime sentence.

What everyone needs to be taught is that the only way to open the door of our inner prison is to act on our own to open the door and let the feelings flow – then the pain ends.

And let's say this right out in the open – the primary need of all children is to feel loved just as they are, and to feel their own love accepted as it flows spontaneously out into other hearts. If parents are healthy at the love level, the child will be also. But what too many children had to do to get any love at all was to twist their natural selves out of shape. And often even that didn't work because the parents were wounded themselves and couldn't provide the needed love to their child.

This condition of constricted and distorted love too often, as mentioned earlier, passes from generation to generation. At some point, the new generation must rise up, say enough of this – and find ways to break free from the family curse. I tell my clients that for me, doing this 'break out' act is actually our responsibility. Only we can heal the curse – so let's do it!

Honest And Responsible

I have a client who came to me about her so-called anger issues. She said her life was a non-stop ugly mess because way too often, she would suddenly fly off the handle for something minor. She soon started talking about her strict sergeant-major of a father. She said she was repeatedly sent to her room and left feeling bad or stupid. When I got her to tap into the underlying feelings she had buried way back then, she was able to get in touch with her buried rage over feeling humiliated in front of her friends, and belittled time and time again by her father. She had tried her best to be what he insisted she be – but still he treated her terribly.

Letting the memory of that anger rise up and wash over her reawakens all the memories and repressed feelings of her rage at her father. In the safety of our therapy room, I helped her to release all that rage – to kick, scream, pound a pillow and finally get all that anger out into the open, and fully accepted by me. And step by step, by getting honest with herself, she began to acknowledge what had happened to her, and then to forgive her tormented father for what he had done. Following that was the process of deepening her self-love and sense of being fully okay, just as she was.

Another client had a problem with her hoarding compulsions. Some researchers believe that hoarding can be related to childhood experiences of losing things. My client told me that she had loved her dog but her mother was always threatening to get rid of it. She then remembered coming home from school one day – and her dog was gone. "Mammy gave away my dog," she told me – and then burst into tears and wild uncontrollable sobs.

Allowing the grief and the tears to flow was very healing for her, because as a child she'd had to stuff all of these feelings of loss away inside her. Now as an adult, she couldn't give anything away, she hoarded compulsively without knowing why. Once she had discharged her pent-up feelings about losing her beloved pet, she was able to stop her hoarding.

Some of us have childhood memories that we look at through rose-colored glasses, fixating on the good memories of what a happy childhood we had, while suppressing and denying all the painful memories. Other people get stuck in the victim perspective and they stay stuck in their victim story. Both of these are unrealistic – and often lead to prolonged repression and adult problems.

What we need to do is to get emotionally honest with ourselves about our childhoods, especially the painful parts.

We need to learn ways to see our past more clearly and get in touch with our emotional wounds. We need to first openly face and accept the old hurt that is still sabotaging our lives. It's estimated that around 85% of a strong emotional reaction is because of old unresolved issues, and only around 15% is related to what is actually happening in present time. And that's a terrible loss of energy in our current lives.

In Robert Burney's book *Codependence: The Dance Of Wounded Souls,* he talks about his own childhood and a short-horn pet calf he named Shorty. Shorty was the closest thing to a deep childhood friend that he had. For two years he developed an emotionally-intimate relationship with that calf – he loved Shorty. The yearling calf became so tame that Robert could sit on his back or crawl under his belly. He spent uncounted hours with that calf. Then came the terrible and totally unexpected disaster:

"I took Shorty to the county fair and got a Blue Ribbon. Then a few weeks later it was time for the show and sale. I got another Blue Ribbon. When it came time to sell him, I had to lead him into the sale ring while the auctioneer sang his mysterious selling chant. It was over in a moment and I let Shorty out of the ring to a pen where all the sold calves were put.

"Somehow I knew that my father expected me not to cry. It was very clear from the role modelling of my father that a man did not cry – ever. I felt suppressed rage at my mother for not protecting me from my father, but I slipped my calf friend's halter off, patted him on the shoulder, and closed the gate, consigning my best friend to the pen of calves that was going to the packing house to be slaughtered.

"No tears for this eight year old. I knew how to be a man. It wasn't until almost 30 years later, leaning up against the side of the AA meeting room that I got the chance to cry for that little boy with great heaving sobs, tears pouring down my cheeks. That was my first experience with deep grief work. I didn't know anything about the process at that time, I just knew that somehow that wounded little boy was still alive inside me. I also didn't know at the time that part of my life's work was going to be helping other people to reclaim the wounded little boys and girls inside them."

He said that the only way for him to start healing his wounds was to go back to that little boy and cry the tears or own the rage that he'd had no permission to own back then. The little boy that he was had felt so betrayed as he was forced to abandon the calf that he loved. He felt guilty for betraying his best friend, even though he'd had zero control over the event.

Another piece of the puzzle was why money had always been such a big issue in his adult life. He said he had a dysfunctional relationship with money in his life – and as he re-examined the terrible trauma of selling his best friend to be slaughtered, he realized that his dysfunctional attitude toward money as an adult had definite roots deep in this childhood trauma. His example might be extreme, but how many of us were pushed into doing things as children that seriously impacted our whole lives? What about you? If you create some space and time, what memories might rise up that are still negatively impacting your current life?

We really have to remember how defenseless and helpless we were back then and how utterly dependent we were on our parents' moods. We were not capable of understanding that our parents might have problems that had nothing to do with us – so it felt like it was all our fault. The inability to love was the parent's problem and was not due to some inherent flaw in the child.

Our lives have been dictated by our wounded inner child. You have to remember it wasn't your fault, you didn't do anything wrong, you were just a kid. We are all carrying around repressed pain, terror, shame and rage energy from our childhoods. So when someone pushes your buttons he/she is activating that stored pressurized grief energy. To think that our early programming has not influenced the way we have lived is to be in denial. Feelings connected with events long ago in childhood can undermine adult relationships, especially if we refuse to even acknowledge their existence.

So let's get honest with ourselves ...

Becoming Vulnerable

Underlying our whole conversation up to this point is the psychological fact that if we don't make ourselves vulnerable, we can't really grow and heal. Emotional vulnerability is defined as the willingness and ability to risk whatever it takes, in order to admit, address, articulate and heal our inner feelings. To be vulnerable means we're exposed, and perhaps open to some sort of attack and damage. To develop emotional vulnerability, we must acknowledge and deal with our emotions, both on our own and in our relationships.

Vulnerability requires both emotional exposure and self-awareness. If we keep ourselves invulnerable to emotional hurt, we can't really be touched emotionally at all – we're perhaps safe, but we can't open up and relate and grow. No one wants to be hurt emotionally, so naturally as children we saw how we got hurt, and found ways to protect ourselves and avoid emotional pain. In essence, we learned how to put on a false front in order to avoid shame, humiliation, rejection, punishment and so forth.

This emerging false front is the personality stance we created in response to those who had power over us in childhood. As we've seen, the false self refers to the neurotic ego and the persona we took on to avoid being vulnerable and hurt any further. We learned very early that it was not always or even ever safe to show our true self. Disapproval from our parents meant our security and happiness might be in jeopardy – so our false self would do whatever it took to win approval and stay safe. The false self is the outfit or suit of armor we put on in order to feel invulnerable and to make life easier.

The false self represents adaptation and conformity. To gain approval we may have had to show only the personality that was acceptable to our parents. Repeated emotional trauma in childhood perhaps caused you to disassociate from your true feelings – and to not be conscious of your authentic emotions at all. Or perhaps you compartmentalized your feelings and hid the unacceptable ones in some place that was invulnerable to exposure and attack. Perhaps you learned to rationalize and deny your unaccepted emotional experiences as 'not you'.

I encourage you to take time and patience to look back honestly and see if any of this rings true for you. Hopefully not – but quite probably at least partially so. This process of emotional disassociation and the formation of a false-self that's impermeable to emotional vulnerability might be serving you quite well in fitting into society, making a good living and even enjoying a picture-perfect family relationship. You might be independent, successful, look the part and be quite popular. But it's a terrible price to pay when you wear a mask and no one knows who you really are.

Perhaps you have convinced yourself that this false front is the true you – but always deep down the false self knows it's hiding the truth – and this causes perpetual anxiety. What if you got found out? Worse still, what if you finally realize that being invulnerable means eternally suffering and living with the feeling of being a phony? I'm not saying this is your present situation. I'm only asking you to honestly get vulnerable and take a look. And then ... own your true self, be responsible for how you're running your inner life – and be brave enough to risk all in order to become your authentic self.

When I begin working with a new client, usually they want to tell me their life story, they want to present me with a narrative that makes sense, that's interesting, that I'll approve of. But I usually cut right to the chase – I want to know what's going on inside them emotionally. I want them to open up, to risk being vulnerable at least with me. Only then can we get right to work dealing with where they really hurt.

Our ego self can spin a great life tale that sounds realistic and reveals how they want to be seen. But that's usually the cover story for a much different life type of past experience. Also, that sort of life story is usually quite boring, revealing only what has been safe for them. Therefore often half-way through this narration I have them pause, tune into their breathing and their whole-body feelings ... and then see what pops up. How are they right now feeling about what they're telling me?

Alice Miller in her book *The Untouched Key* says she did her Thesis on Friedrich Nietzsche, whose adult writings reflect the unlived feelings, needs and tragedy of his childhood. His father strictly forbade him from ever expressing certain feelings, and severely punished him when he did. Then at age four his father died, and soon thereafter his brother died as well. Friedrich was left as the only male in a household of women – his grandmother, two aunts, mother, and younger sister.

Nietzsche's mother, who was only eighteen when he was born, is described by biographers as cold, stupid and disinterested. His strict upbringing by these women, who practiced stern inhibited Christian virtues, left Nietzsche questioning the values of such virtues when there was no love present in the household. "What good are these virtues," he later wrote, "for I am 'the neighbor' you're supposed to love?" Miller speaks of Nietzsche as a defenseless child who was emotionally and physically punished and at the same time forbidden to defend himself, to cry, to scream, to rage – he was a child from whom only obedience and good behavior was allowed.

Nietzsche suffered from chronic throat infections which were probably a way of compensating for the screams he was forbidden to express. Finally at the age of 45 the pain he had carried in him for so long broke through. On a peaceful street in Turin, Italy, in January 1889 Nietzsche watched a coachman brutally whipping his horse. Nietzsche threw himself between them, and threw his arms around the horse's neck to defend the horse from the blows. And overcome by his rising anger and sadness, he finally burst into tears.

The man who has spent his life suppressing the feelings of an abused child was finally weeping uncontrollably. Alice Miller states "if Nietzsche had not been forced to learn as a child that one must master an 'unbearable fit of sobbing', if he had simply been *allowed* to sob as a child, then humanity would perhaps have been one philosopher poorer – but in return the life of a human being named Nietzsche would have been richer. And who knows what that *vital* Nietzsche would then have been able to give humanity?"

CONCLUSION

Growing up I didn't learn a language that could express my feelings. I thought that being emotionally vulnerable was being weak. But in fact vulnerability reflects authenticity, truthfulness and transparency. Vulnerability fosters genuineness and builds trust in relationships, plus resilience and self-confidence. Vulnerability bring to light all our feelings, so we can process them. It is the only way toward authentic and meaningful connections with others, and with our own selves.

CHAPTER SIX

Are You Waiting To Be Happy?

~~~~~~

If I could live my life over, I wish I had learned early on to not be afraid of my feelings – to stop waiting and start living. And I wish I had tapped much earlier into the power of my attention. I wish I had known from childhood on that I am a creator and I have the power to manifest. And I wish I had known that worrying is wasted energy.

The Top Six Regrets Of The Dying:

> *I wish I had been true to myself and not live the life that others expected of me.*
>
> *I wish I hadn't spent so much of my time working so hard and being caught up in the rat race.*
>
> *I wish I'd been more connected to my emotions and had the courage to express my true feelings.*
>
> *I wish I had stayed in touch with my friends and not let friendships slip away over the years.*
>
> *I wish I had taken more risks when I had the chance and not stayed stuck in my comfort zone, sticking with my familiar habits and patterns.*
>
> *I wish I had not been so afraid of change.*

I remember how I would buy a new stylish outfit and put it in the wardrobe and say "I'll keep that for special occasions." I'd wear other clothes I had when going out, as I was keeping the
~~~~~~

new one for that special occasion. Then in a year or two the outfit had gone out of fashion. Then I'd think of the price I'd paid for that and lament that I never got the wear out of it. Why? Because I was waiting for the really special occasions.

So – now I wear my best outfits whenever I am invited anywhere. I've learned that life is for living ... for living right now. Nothing is waiting, this is it. This present moment is not life waiting to happen. I remember in my Nanna's house she used to have a nice sitting room in her house. We only got to be in this room at Christmastime when she would take out her best china set from the glass cabinet. The rest of the year that good room and that good china would be locked away while we would all be cramped into her everyday little sitting room. What a waste.

Well – what are you waiting for?

Waiting to meet the man or woman of your dreams?

Waiting to lose weight?

Waiting till the kids grow up?

Waiting to get divorced?

Waiting to retire?

Waiting to be more qualified?

Waiting to win the lotto?

Waiting for your partner to change?

Waiting for an apology?

Waiting for a pay rise or a promotion?

Waiting till the time is right?

Waiting for the big break?

Waiting for your elderly parents to die?

Waiting on your inheritance?

Waiting to be discovered?

Waiting to get rich?

Waiting to write that book?

Waiting for him/her to propose?

Waiting for your next holiday?

Waiting for enlightenment?

Waiting to die?

I challenge you to put down this book right now and answer honestly this question: *WHAT AM I WAITING FOR?*

The message here is very clear –
stop waiting and start living.

With my clients I've found that most of them are waiting for something. And while they're waiting basically their life is on hold. They don't usually realize the time they've wasted in waiting. Instead they have become addicted to the mindset of waiting. I recall an acquaintance of mine who was waiting for her mother-in-law to die so that she could inherit and clear her large debts. Everything was hinged on getting this big inheritance. But the mother-in-law is still alive and my friend's life is still on hold. I wonder if this person ever looks back at her life and sees all the missed opportunities she let pass her by while she was in waiting mode.

It seems that most people are waiters. A lot of them are waiting to meet their soul mate and are meanwhile feeling miserable being single, telling themselves that when they meet their soul mate they'll finally feel happy and complete. But in my observation we never reach a point in our life where everything is solved and wonderful. There is no final perfect scene – there's just the continual life journey. Waiting is such a trap. It robs us of our life, our present-moment sense of joy and fulfillment.

Waiting is a form of non-acceptance of where we are right now. Waiting is putting the present on hold till we get what we're waiting for in the future. The world's greatest hold on us is the false promise of a perfect tomorrow. We're not 'here' because we're chronically waiting to be 'there'.

All I can say is – look at your waiting-situation ... and then choose to put an end to it. Drop the waiting and you'll suddenly feel lighter and brighter. The future will disappear and the present moment will light up! Nothing ever happens in the future – it only happens in the present moment. Waiting is whittling your precious time away. A lot of people spend the whole year waiting for their two-week holiday in the summer time. They say that looking forward to their vacation is what keeps them going. Or maybe they work their butt off during the prime years of their life, just waiting to retire and be happy. In my observation, that's a false and tragic forecast.

Ask the question of yourself: are you just trudging along mindlessly toward your retirement, feeling mostly unhappy while waiting to be happy then? The solution is clear: choose to be happy now, regardless of your life situation. Here's a classic story you've perhaps heard before, but it's worth retelling because it's so to the point.

The Mexican Fisherman

An American investment banker was at the pier of a small coastal Mexican village when a small rustic boat with just one fisherman approached the shore and docked. The American complimented the Mexican on the quality of his fish and asked how long it took to catch them. The Mexican replied, not long. The American then asked why didn't he stay out longer and catch more fish? The Mexican said he had enough to support his family so he didn't need to catch any more.

The American then asked the fisherman what he did with the rest of his time. The Mexican said, "I relax, play with my children, enjoy siestas with my wife, and in the evenings we stroll into the village, sip wine and play some tunes with our friends."

The American said, "I am a Harvard MBA and could show you how to make more money and live a better life. You should spend more time fishing, and with the extra proceeds buy a bigger boat, with the money you'll make with the bigger boat you could buy several boats, hire employees and eventually own a fleet of boats and run your own fishing company. Instead of selling your fish to a middle man, you could negotiate directly with the processing plants and a large distributor – and maybe even open up your own plant. You could then leave this little village and move to Mexico City or even New York and oversee your huge enterprise. You'd be a great success!"

The Mexican fisherman responded patiently: "But how long will all this take?" "Maybe 15 to 20 years," the American replied. "But what then?" asked the Mexican. The American laughed and said: "That's the best part. When the time is right you could then sell your company and become very rich, you could make millions and retire, move to a quiet town on the coast and enjoy your life." To which the wise Mexican fisherman replied, "What do you think I'm doing now?"

I so love that story.

Most people are striving all their lives to finally get somewhere, and in the meantime they forget to pay attention to where they actually are right now. The best things in life are always found right here. We are so often surrounded by a breath-taking moment that we simply don't notice because our attention is focused on the future, not the present. There are so many bright wonders in our lives that go unnoticed and unrecognized as we busily forge our way forward. Just the feeling of being alive and relatively healthy inside our own marvelous bodies is such a blessing! But instead of living and loving now, we spend our time striving for better times in the future. Then we tell ourselves we'll be happy.

When someone we love dies and we look back on that relationship, usually it's not the big major events that we fondly remember – it's all the momentary and seemingly-insignificant moments. Our fondest memories are about those special moments that we shared with someone, experiences and feelings that we didn't recognize as being important at the time. When my husband died, a memory that comes back to me often is when we were attending a concert in the Point Theatre in Dublin, his home city.

The band was playing one of our favorite songs, "Everybody's Changing", and my husband spontaneously stood up and started dancing. I remember smiling at him, seeing how happy he was dancing to that song he loved. When I think of him now, that memory often pops into my mind. Little did I know at the time that this would be a memory that would stick with me forever. It wasn't a big special occasion like our wedding day – it was that simple moment at that concert.

We must remember that life is a journey, not a destination. Life is a process, and being in process is not just about the end result. It's about experiencing what's happening each moment, all along the way. We're all so rich in experience – but only if we pay attention and stop being lost in thoughts about the past and future. Yes, we can create wonderful imaginations about how things are going to be at some point later in our lives – but there's no substitute, happiness-wise, for the actual feelings we experience in our bodies right now.

What is happiness anyway? A concept, an imagination that we hope will somehow appear if we manage our lives just right? It's said that happiness is fleeting and that's true. We can't sustain those sudden feelings of joy and fulfillment that appear and then disappear just as fast as they came to us. Doesn't it seem wise to focus where true happiness lives, here and now? So why do we try to grasp a moment of happiness, squeezing it to death in the process? Isn't it a better choice to fully enjoy and then willingly let go of a joyful happy moment, so that we can be open to the next moment of joy?

This comes down to a basic fact of life. We can either manipulate our lives, trying to make things become the way we want them to be – or we can spontaneously participate in life, accepting the natural flow we're engaged in. We can't really do both at the same time. Manipulation separates us from the world. Participation immerses us in life. And really, where is happiness to be found? In feeling fully engaged in the current flow of life.

See if you can often each day, pause and consider if you're working selfishly to manipulate things to your advantage, or surrendering to the larger flow of life – participating rather than manipulating. And notice which of these, manipulation or participation, brings you true happiness. Of course we need to manipulate to a certain extent – but we need to also ease up, surrender to the moment emerging right now ... and allow happiness to sneak up behind us and bless us with its uplifting touch.

The United States of America has in its Bill of Rights "the pursuit of happiness". This seems slightly off the mark. We can't chase and grab happiness. We can't pursue happiness and possess it. But we can focus regularly where happiness is to be found, here and now – and be thankful when it comes our way. Life has its ups and downs. If we accept all of life, there's always plenty of happiness to enjoy along our winding path.

Have you ever done a mountain-hike? The intention at the beginning of the hike is to get to the peak and experience the spectacular mountain views. But it's equally important to enjoy all the natural beauty along the trail, soak in the presence of the plants and wild flowers along the way. Perhaps halfway up the mountain there comes a sudden rain shower and you have to turn back – it doesn't mean you failed because you didn't get to see the mountain-view. Overall, if you spent four hours hiking and ten minutes up on the top, where will most of the pleasure be found?

Tomorrow, tomorrow, I love you tomorrow.
You're only a day away.

From the musical *Annie*

I like to give little assignments to my clients – things to do each day between sessions. If they do these things, they accelerate their progress along the path. As you've seen, I've been doing this in this book as well. And here's a good one to do each day until it becomes a positive habit:

Just pause for a few breaths, get grounded in your breathing and your whole body – and ask yourself the following question: "Am I living right now ... or am I wishing my life away, waiting for the good times to come?"

You have really only one moment in your hands – this moment right now. And either you open up and fully experience it or you leave it unlived, waiting on the promise of tomorrow.

ANTICIPATION VERSUS WAITING

The film *The Shawshank Redemption* illustrated this theme of fully living in the moment with the quote: "Get busy living or get busy dying." Bob Dylan said it similarly with: "He not busy being born is busy dying." Andy Dufresne (Tim Robbins) in the film wasn't just waiting to get out of prison. He was literally chipping away in his cell every night with his rock hammer, working toward his escape. The anticipation of escaping empowered his present moment into action. And in the meantime, look at all the good he did for the men in the prison with him. He set up a library for them to enjoy reading, he introduced music for them to listen to. He tutored one young man to pass his high school diploma. He even called the whole prison to a halt one day by playing beautiful music through the loudspeakers.

When Andy did escape, all the other prisoners told endless stories about him to new inmates – because Andy had made such a positive impression on them. Even when in prison he was living in the moment, not in the future, and making the best of his surroundings and helping the people he was with. And yet he was also planning and anticipating his escape. What he wasn't doing, in contrast to his fellow inmates, was just passively waiting.

Do not wait –
the time will never be 'just right' –
start where you stand and work with
whatever tools you have at your command.
Better tools will be found as you go along.

Napoleon Hill

If today was unexpectedly your last day on planet Earth, it would be such a tragedy if you hadn't fully been here and experienced the multitude of vivid instantaneous sensory inputs that had come flowing into you through your eyes, ears, nose and bodily sensations, plus all the various emotional flows. If out of habit you'd spent most of your time fixated on the promise of tomorrow, on your deathbed you'll deeply miss all the lost possibilities of that last day. I don't mean to overwork this point – but because most of us have such strong 'waiting' habits, we do need to strongly reinforce the power and glory of living here now, not there then. Just drop the whole idea of 'I'll Be Happy When ...'

It also bears repeating that the neurotic ego wants you to believe that your happiness isn't going to be found here and now, it's to be found just around the corner. If you're content and happy in the moment you won't have much need of your past-future fixated ego, and that's what a neurotic ego most fears – losing your attention, and therefore fading into the background of your life.

So yes – you're going to encounter ego resistance to what we're talking about here. Our whole economic system is based on pursuing happiness, not relaxing into it. Of course we need a healthy ego to help us gain and sustain the life we want. But we surely don't need an ego that's chronically anxious or depressed – after all, happiness cannot be found in those negative fear-based mindsets. Therefore the ego needs some re-education.

So regularly take some time to self-talk with your ego. Expect it to freak out when you even slightly consider what we're talking about in this book. Just keep raising the logical argument that in order to have the life you need, you need to tone down all the worried thoughts and apprehensions the ego keeps fixating on, and spend more time in the here and now where happiness can come to brighten your moods.

Definitely allow your ego to feel needed when certain actions are required, we do need to get ourselves to work and pay the bills and so forth. But also let your ego know that you no longer want it to dominate, to control, to pollute your present-moment experience with all its future worries. Begin to focus deeper within than your ego mind can go. Get out of your thinking head and down into your heart and gut where real living takes place. Yeah!

There is a pub in Australia that I visited once which had a sign in their garden that read:

FREE BEER HERE TOMORROW

But of course that tomorrow never comes. Each day you turn up for that free beer, only to realize that the promise of the free beer is once again for tomorrow.

Waiting is passive. Anticipation is active. It's a paradox that we must work for our daily bread (or beer) and a more-or-less secure tomorrow – and at the same time we must relax and open up to the fullness of each new moment. Paradoxes abound deeper down in human life. And often the solution is in finding a healthy fulfilling balance between two extremes.

We all know how hard it is to quiet our chatterbox ego minds. And I'm not suggesting that you go around all day with no thoughts in your mind. What I am suggesting is working to form a habit of stopping even for a few breaths during your busy day, to just do nothing – except experience! Mindfulness meditation is a great help in doing this. Just refocus your mind's attention down into your breathing experience. Expand that awareness to include your heart. And expand that experience to include all the various sensations arising from your bodily presence in the here and now ... and dwell in that joyful experience adequately to where you regain your senses, empower your true self, and set your mind and soul free ...

CONCLUSION

I wasted many precious years being in waiting mode – waiting for the love and approval of my parents, waiting for my plans to be perfect before I implement them, waiting till the time was just right to do certain things. Then I realized that the time is never just right – we've just got to jump in and do it. As Oscar Wilde once said: "Youth is wasted on the young." Most of us go to extraordinary lengths to ignore or deny the fact that we are going to one day die. So we live focused on the future.

But death does come. There will come an end to this remarkable experience of being alive in an amazing vibrant body that can feel such pleasure and happiness, as well as all the down moods of life. It's not being morbid to think about how our life is a temporary situation. To fully embrace our death is to fully embrace life. Jesus said something that rings so true: "The kingdom of heaven is at hand." This is it, as Alan Watts once said.

I feel we all have a responsibility to live our lives to the utmost. That's why I'm a life coach. Stephen Levine wrote a book called *A Year To Live*. He committed himself to living a year as though it were his last – and to be fully alive. In the book he asks the question: If you had only one year to live, what would you do? Would you carry on with your usual habits and moods? Or would you stop waiting and risk everything in order to feel more vibrant and appreciated and fulfilled?

I encourage you to reflect on this deeply ...

Also – if you were to live your life over, what parts would you want to change? How much of your time, energy and resources have you wasted in waiting for something to happen before you could be happy?

I feel that each of us bears within our hearts and souls a call. When we are in tune with ourselves we follow this call – and it's usually a call that's bigger than our egos think we are. If we wait till we're on our deathbed before we review our lives, it's too late – and that is indeed a tragedy all around. It seems wise to learn how to tap into our call, respond to it with all our heart and soul, and then act to apply our unique gift to benefit the world. Let's not cheat the world by waiting all our lives before contributing – let's right now start giving what we have to give. That in fact is where real happiness is to be found.

Personally, after waiting years and years I'm finally answering the call to write this book. The more important a call or action is to our evolution, of course the more resistance we might feel toward pursuing our call – but let's not succumb to a life of regret because the path sometimes gets rough. Let's jump in and do the work we are meant to do.

CHAPTER SEVEN

Worry Is A Wasted Emotion

~~~~~~~~~~~~~~~~~~~~~~~~~~~~~~~

Do you lie awake at night agonizing over things that could happen? Do you automatically expect the worst – are you an obsessive worrier? Worrying like waiting is best approached as a disease of the mind. Another name for worry could be fear-based undisciplined thinking. When we worry we can't stop ourselves from obsessing over an issue that seems to be looming threateningly in our personal future.

Worrying has been documented to almost never help us navigate a difficult situation. Why? Because worrying pushes our anxiety buttons – and when we're anxious our brains don't function rationally. Also, when we're anxious our creative powers, as we saw earlier, become dull. This means we can't find creative solutions to what's making us worry. All worrying does is sap us of the energy we'll need to deal with a threat.

So why is our whole culture caught up in chronic worrying and anxiety? One culprit is tech. Things are changing so fast, most of us simply can't stay on top of all the tech advances. Also, we're constantly being bombarded with fearful things in the media. If it's not war it's disease. If it's not micro-plastic pollution found in babes in the womb, it's floods and fires and global ecological disasters. No wonder we're all getting more and more worried about the future!

And here's perhaps the worst of it all. People with PhDs in psychology have been studying what attracts human attention the strongest – and corporations hire them to do just that.
~~~~~~~~~~~~~~~~~~~~~~~~~~~~~~~

Unfortunately for our peace of mind, our brains come prewired to be heads-up for danger of any kind. No matter what we're focused on, if we perceive danger we instantly shift our full attention in that direction. Aha! So if a media company puts up threatening content, viewers are going to watch that program.

Just turn on the news – voila. Almost zero non-anxious content. Turn on a soap or night-time drama and it's the same. Constant danger, threatening relationship situations, and almost always, dangerous people out doing bad things. Doom and gloom almost always win out over relaxed peaceful shows. And it's almost like we can't help it as viewer – we need to stay alert to danger, but in the process we get continually stimulated to worry all the time.

In a very real way, we should hold advertising agencies and corporations accountable for the acute mental-health situation we're in worldwide. Their fear-based programming has already turned us into chronic-anxiety victims. We're being taken advantage of – our ancient survival instincts are being manipulated in order to make the corporations richer and richer. Our political leaders know this full well – but they're not doing anything about it. Instead the medical community is making literally trillions of dollars on prescription drugs that really don't help much at all to dampen our debilitating anxiety.

What can we actually do to reduce our own worries? First of all we can become more discerning about what we watch on TV and on our media feeds. Maybe we like the rush of excitement that stimulates our bodies when watching violent and overly-dramatic shows – but we need to evaluate the price we're paying in our peace of mind and mental health. We can just say no – turn the channel or better still, turn off that chronic source of negative stimulation. Keep a minimal eye on the news – but if you can't do anything about it, don't obsess about it.

Worry is not a part of our natural make up. Seeing an immediate danger, feeling a rush of fear and then using that charge to deal with the danger – yes, this is good! But worrying isn't a present-moment emotion. It's all future-fixated. Your dog or cat or the bird out your window doesn't sit around worrying about tomorrow or next week. Unless humans torture and condition animals to be constantly anxious, animals just aren't. And when animals are conditioned to live in constant fear, what happens? They tend to get sick and die.

But here's the hope for us humans. We have minds that can observe a negative situation and then deduce a solution to the problem. We can make rational choices and act on them. A lot of a life coach's job is helping clients realize they do have choices. And one of the main things we can do is choose not to worry. Worrying leads to the feeling of victimization – but don't be fooled. You're not a victim here.

Well, actually you're a victim until you realize what's going on, and do something to change it. And first of all in this wake-up process, we need to follow any of our worries back to its root source. Always our worries are grounded in the ultimate fear that if worse comes to worst, we're going to get killed or otherwise die because of the threat we face. Even if it's purely imaginary or something happening on TV, our minds and bodies react as if we're in mortal danger – so darn right, we've got something to worry about.

And here's another thing about fear – our bodies and the fear-center of our brain can't tell the difference between a real danger and an imagined one – this is well proven, and it's a crucial fact when deciding to reduce your worrying. This is why media inputs that stimulate the human fear response are so effective in holding our attention. As soon as we detect a danger, real or not, we're going to keep watching in that direction. So sure, go ahead and watch media inputs that scare or threaten you and thus give you an adrenaline rush – but stay keenly aware that you're increasing your worry quota.

And how about the ways you chronically scare your own self? The human mind is amazing in its power to imagine all sorts of things. This is a marvelous ability – but once again, it wasn't designed to function in the high-stimulation world we now live in. Our minds can conjure up the most horrible scenarios in our imagination – and our primitive fear-center of the brain can't tell the difference between our imagined horror and the real thing. And so we're continually scaring ourselves!

What do you worry about the most? Financial disaster, physical injury, disease, loneliness, natural disaster, old age, war, death? Even without an external stimulant regarding any one of these, your mind will habitually start worrying about something threatening your wellbeing – and off you go in your imagination, worrying yourself to death but not really resolving the situation – because you're worrying about something possibly happening in the future, not something you can deal with in the present moment.

Worrying will add nothing to your life. So don't waste your time and energy in futile worrying. There are a number of successful programs that life coaches guide their clients through, and many books that are helpful as well, and online programs also. But it's your choice to act in this direction. If you're a worrier and suffering as a result – act! And the first act is to begin watching your own mind in action. Watch a worried thought pop into your mind. Look to see where it came from. Follow it back to its roots – and discover that you're actually worrying about your own possible future demise – about dying.

Again – dealing with your unavoidable ultimate demise as a living organism on this earth is one of the keys to living a happy life. Ignoring or denying your own mortality is in fact the root cause of anxiety and worry. So hey, begin to look honestly at who you really are, and how you're at some point going to cease to exist. Get used to the idea. Learn to accept reality at this level – it's the shortest route to less worry and more enjoyment of the time you have left on Earth.

Worrying is like a rocking chair.
It gives you something to do
but it gets you nowhere.

Glenn Turner

Be Careful What You Wish For

I had a client who told me she was a born worrier. As a child she was worried about the boogie man lurking beneath her bed, as a teenager she worried about her school test results, as a college student she worried about failing her degree, and now as a worker she worries about losing her job. I mentioned to her a book I had recently read, Viktor Frankl's *Man's Search for Meaning*. A famous quote from that book is:

Everything can be taken from a man but one thing,
the last of the human freedoms:
to choose one's attitude in any given circumstance –
to choose one's own way.

I pointed out to her that worrying was actually a choice. Frankl said: "*Between stimulus and response there is a space, and in that space is our power to choose our response – and in our response lies our growth and our freedom.*"

Our wishes in life are often an opposite reflection of what we're afraid will happen. We wish for loads of money because we're afraid we'll end up with nothing. We wish for a deep relationship because we're afraid of being lonely. We wish for good health because we fear illness and death. The Bible expresses this succinctly:

For the thing which I greatly feared
is come upon me –
and that which I was afraid of
is come unto me.

Remember you are a creative being, and your thoughts are the creative agent busy manifesting your visions, dreams, worries and so forth. I sometimes feel that worrying about something is actually like putting in a request to the universe and asking for it to happen. There is no worry in nature, as we discussed before. Humans are the thinkers – and we reap what we sow.

I often said I should have named my dog 'Ruby The Path Of Least Resistance' because he always found the easiest way to enjoy life. If it was a really hot summer day I'd find Ruby in the shadiest place in the garden. Then in the winter when a beam of sunlight would be shining in the window on the sofa or the mat, there I'd find Ruby basking in the sunlight. I left Ruby in a friend's house one day. The woman didn't like dogs in her house so she put him out in her back garden. She had a clothes line full of bed clothes out drying. When I came to collect Ruby there he was in the middle of her garden asleep on one of her duvet covers which he'd pulled off the line. Needless to say my friend was not impressed but that scene did bring a smile to my face. Ruby didn't worry about the future – he engaged successfully with the present.

If you are worried that there is a boogie man in your wardrobe, shine a light in the wardrobe and see the truth. That's the end of the worrying. Deal with the worry – and be done with it.

So let's say a problem arises. Your flat mate announces suddenly she is leaving. You can't afford the rent on your own, so you feel worried. But instead of going into frozen anxiety you can catch yourself worrying – and choose to act rather than worry. There's always something you can do if you put aside worry and apply that energy toward finding a solution. Sometimes the resolution is right before you – you heard yesterday about someone seeking a new apartment with a roommate – make the phone call rather than worrying.

Also, insight and inspiration can't arise when anxiety is present. Hope is the opposite of anxiety – so focus on aiming your current attention toward the feeling of hope. Remember times when you were anxious and you pushed beyond the frozen state and resolved the dilemma – look to the positive outcome you want. Something will happen, you might decide to post an ad or talk with friends – reach out!

But watch yourself. Don't just passively wish for a miracle – instead formulate your wish realistically, and decide to take realistic action. Identify the nagging tension in your gut – listen to it but don't instantly let it push worry buttons that'll weaken your resolve and let your overly-imaginative mind run away with worst case scenarios. Again – if you practice a number of times choosing to stay hopeful with little things, when the big shockers come you can immediately say to yourself, hey, I refuse to sink into anxiety. I'm going to focus on making steps to move beyond the challenge I'm facing.

When we start worrying we are then not thinking about the action to be taken. When a client comes for coaching and they go on and on about a problem, after a while I ask them what they are going to do about their dilemma, what action steps can they take? Too often they have no idea because they haven't logically thought the whole thing through – they're too emotional and contracted to think straight.

I then guide them through the process of observing the pattern of their anxious mind – and show them that if they manage their thoughts successfully, they can always at least see one tiny step they can make in the right direction. And they then can discover for themselves that every time they go into action, commit to taking a baby step, one of three things will happen: they'll take the step and it moves them forward, and they can then see the next step to take; they'll take a step and it moves them backward, and they learn a good lesson; or they take a baby step that generates a breakthrough that would never have happened if they hadn't taken the baby step.

Here's another thing: each time you sink into worry mode, you limit yourself to a narrow focus in your life – the problem you're worrying about. If you're worried about money and immediately exclude everything else, you'll think your money worries are your whole life – and the worry will consume you. You become identified with it and unable to stand back and see the bigger picture. Get grounded in your deeper sense of who you are and what you're here to do ... and so often a solution will arise.

If you were to crash your car, you'd probably see this problem-solution process in action. You don't just sit there frozen in anxiety, at least not for long. Instead you instinctively go into gear and do the first thing you see to do – open the car door, see if you're injured, get out and seek help, etc. All you have to do is respond to events as they occur, and keep on problem solving. In my experience what is necessary will be provided by the natural unfolding of events. The primary secret is not to succumb to the mental process of worrying. All you accomplish with your worrying is delaying the action needed for the solution.

If you were told you had cancer and had a month to live, watch every problem, every worry, all of your unhappiness drop away, vanish into thin air. You would see that life is always good right now. When we take action worry disappears. Often when we finally pluck up the courage to meet a problem head on, the problem simply disappears or gets resolved. When we develop the courage to have that difficult conversation, make that dreaded phone call, confront that employee, the problem evaporates. Foreboding is gone. Life can flow again.

I don't mean to paint an over-pretty picture of all this. And I don't mean to imply that you should just count on magic to resolve your worries. Ingrained patterns of worrying are often inherited from our parents and they run deep. Part of the reason I became a therapist and life coach was because I saw how hard it was in my own life to overcome anxiety patterns. But I also saw that with the right tools, timing and intentions, there is not only hope but almost a certainty that most people can overcome a worried mind

So wish for gaining a pragmatic approach and guidance for transcending your worries. Sure, they'll sometimes still raise their ugly heads and drag you down temporarily. But once you learn the basic process for shifting from anxiety to determination and action, you'll be able to catch your worry mode early on, spotlight it – and move beyond it into clarity and action.

Look At The Birds

While I was writing this chapter on worry I got a text on my phone giving me a code number for a purchase which I hadn't made being charged on my debit card. I admit my first reaction was total panic. OMG, is someone emptying my bank account? Then I caught myself reacting, and told myself – now Linda, practice what you preach. Take a deep breath, recover your perspective – this isn't the end of the world. It's not a life-or-death situation. So I made the first step toward solving the problem. I went into action and rang the Fraud Department of my bank. While stuck on hold waiting in a queue to get a Fraud Agent, I realized the next step I should make. I went into my 24-hour banking and transferred the money from my current compromised account into my savings account. I then got an agent on the phone who immediately cancelled the card, and gave me instructions on what to do next. All sorted out.

If that had happened to me a few years ago I would have been so anxious and irrational that I would have gone totally into panic mode. I'm so thankful that I have learned to push aside my old panic reaction, give clear thought to the problem and then take the appropriate action. When we worry, we lose control of our mind. Our neurotic ego freaks out and thinks irrational thoughts that can lead to disaster. Worrying in essence takes us out of the only mindset from which we can actually fix the problem.

One of my favorite quotes from the Bible is found in the Gospel of Matthew 6:25-34. I am going to paraphrase it:

Don't worry about having something to eat, drink, or wear. Isn't life more than food or clothing? Look at the birds in the sky, they don't plant or harvest, they don't even store grain in barns. Yet your father in Heaven takes care of them.

Aren't you worth more than birds? Can worry make you live longer? Look how the wild flowers grow – they don't work hard to make themselves beautiful or handsome. But I tell you, Solomon with all his wealth wasn't as well clothed as is a flower in bloom. Our Creator gives such beauty to everything that grows in the fields, even though it is here today and thrown into the oven tomorrow – and surely the same is true for us.

Jesus owned nothing more than a set of clothes to wear, and yet he led perhaps the most fulfilled life that anybody has ever lived. And if we live each new day fully in the present moment, it does seem that our future will unfold accordingly.

CONCLUSION

I wasted over six years of my life worrying over a court case I was caught up in. If I'd had the mindset I have now, I would not have spent a minute worrying. Most legal cases take years to be resolved as they run their course. And I realized after those wasted anxious years that worrying brought nothing to the table. Worrying makes no sense at all. Worrying has no benefit whatsoever – it's a very bad habit. As we've seen, it takes us out of the mindset where we can fix the problem, and meanwhile it sucks our creative problem-solving energy.

Worrying is actually focusing in the wrong direction. Our minds are so powerful that focusing on what we don't want to happen can actually bring it about. "The thing which I greatly feared has come upon me." By telling you not to worry I'm not talking about going into denial about an actual problem in your life. Instead you can look at the problem dispassionately, decide on a specific course of action – and apply it. Detach yourself from the problem so that it doesn't sap your creative power. And yes, have faith that there is meaning and purpose and love in the world, and that you can confidently participate in that present-moment flow of life.

We do have the inner power and higher intuitive guidance to evaluate a problem without worrying about it. Worrying is actually the biggest obstacle to solving the problem. Always remember that worrying is a choice, it's a bad choice, a wasted emotion. How much precious time have you wasted worrying? And do you feel ready to break out of that pattern?

CHAPTER EIGHT

Your Yin/Yang Balance

~~~~~~~~~~~~~~~~~~~~~~~~~~~~

Around a hundred years ago, the Swiss psychologist Carl Jung dedicated much of his life to the study of the unconscious – that part of the mind containing memories, associations and impulses that the individual is not aware of. One of Jung's main observations was that deep within each person there is what he called their Anima and their Animus. He drew the terms, and also the general concept, both from his own experience, the accounts of his clients, and from ancient Greek myths. The core theme was that all human beings are always looking for our 'other half' which we can subtly sense exists buried inside us within what Jung called the unconscious.

It's well documented that male and female humans share almost identical DNA. The DNA sequence of any two individuals is about 99.9% identical. The remaining 0.1% accounts for the genetic variations that make each person unique. Therefore it's logical that Jung was right – we are both male and female deep-down in our genes. For the first two months in the womb, the embryo is entirely female – then half of the female embryos turn sexually into male embryos.
~~~~~~~~~~~~~~~~~~~~~~~~~~~~

But ... overall we're actually a balance of female and male. And it seems that women unconsciously seek to encounter and integrate their male side, and men unconsciously seek to merge with their female side. Jung explored this dynamic in depth, and greatly helped in our understanding of otherwise-strange unconscious experiences. In my work I find an exploration of this inner dynamic vital to true self-discovery.

In ancient Chinese/Taoist traditions we also find this focus on the male/female balance. The term 'yin' refers to our inner, female, soft, yielding, nurturing qualities, and the term 'yang' refers to our external, hard, forceful, dominating qualities. Obviously we all have these qualities, but sometimes they get out of balance and a person is much more yin than yang, or more yang than yin.

Just off the cuff, would you say in general you're more yang or more yin? There's no right or wrong with this – it's okay to be either regardless of your physical sex. But often in self-discovery it's important to look openly and see where you might be blocking your yin or yang energies – and learn to open up that energy and integrate it into your personality. Great expansions in a person's life can occur when a buried yin or yang quality and energy is released and allowed to blossom in one's life.

Jung worked with the term Anima for yin, and Animus for yang. Anima development in a man is related to the male opening up to deep-felt 'soft' emotions such as intuitive processes, creative expression, imagination, and heightened sensitivity and empathy toward himself and others. Animus development in a woman is all about the woman (or yin man) opening up to express courage, determination and a willingness to face challenges, and to venture out in the world. In Jung's writings, Anima is thought to be the feminine part of a man's soul and the Animus refers to the masculine part of a female's soul.

A person is in balance when they have a good relationship with both their masculine and feminine selves. The indwelling masculine and feminine energies that we all possess are ancient archetypes or raw forms of energy that every being contains regardless of gender. The term *androgyny* has its roots in classical mythology and literature. Androgyny comes from the Greek words *andros* meaning 'man' and *gyn* meaning 'woman' – an androgynous person is therefore one who has both masculine and feminine characteristics.

You've probably seen the ancient yin-yang symbol of a circle with a black (yin) and a white (yang) inner figure representing the father-mother Creator, with the Creator thus being androgynous. At all levels in the universe, this balance of yin and yang, male and female, positive charge and negative charge reigns supreme. In Jungian terms the integration of the opposites within oneself is dominant – the bringing together of the male and female energies and qualities and expressions within the individual human psyche.

I like to think of these energies as frequencies. To function in wholeness and balance within ourselves, the two opposites must be balanced. When I'm coaching clients I rely considerably on my feminine side – being receptive and holding a safe nurturing space for my clients. When I'm out doing marketing for my business, or negotiating a training deal, I am more in my masculine side – being proactive and putting myself out in the world. Depending on the situation, we need to get comfortable with both our feminine and masculine sides – and often this can take considerable work to achieve.

A World Out Of Balance

I'd say that our human presence on this planet has been quite out of balance for thousands of years now. We have placed enormous value on the masculine paradigm – the world of logic, rationality, manipulation, dominance, forcefulness, solution-focused thinking. The dominance of masculine energy is everywhere. We're still living in a patriarchal society where the feminine paradigm has been undervalued, disrespected and suppressed ... big time. The violent unfair rape-and-pillage condition of our current world order is an obvious expression of this.

Meanwhile the divine feminine has been demeaned, removed from her rightful place of reverence, and downplayed. There have been times and cultures when there were gods and goddesses and all was equal and in balance. Certain so-called primitive tribes still maintain this equilibrium between yin and yang. But most of us live in a masculine-dominated society where yang traits are celebrated while feminine traits are considered lesser and dismissed. The dominant religions over the ages have felt threatened by the power of the divine feminine.

Take Mary Magdalene from the stories in the Bible for instance. In the early Christian Church, she seems to have held a much more prominent role than we have been led to believe over the centuries. The Gnostic Gospels speak of Mary Magdalene as the principle disciple of Jesus, described as "the woman who knew all things". She was the apostle endowed with knowledge, vision and insight far exceeding the others. She was even talked about as "the twin flame of Jesus" and together they shared a profound and deep love.

But then, based on jealousy and fear of the power of the feminine, especially the kind of power that she had, the male-dominated Catholic Church branded Mary Magdalene as a whore and prostitute and cut her out of their hierarchy. Ever since, in both Catholic and Protestant Churches, male dominance has persevered – resulting in many generations where it's been assumed that male dominance is the way of God, not equality among yin and yang. Male dominance in other religions has been equally pernicious – ask any Islamic woman.

Men and women do unconsciously possess both masculine and feminine energies in almost equal balance. When we disown or cut off one side of ourselves, the resulting imbalance will inevitably over time result in, well – what we have today. So in our world culture we must make a concerted effort to regain this ultimate yin-yang balance, in politics and government, commerce, family life, religious life – life in general. And from my understanding we must start within our own selves – that's the only path to universal balance.

For instance we have got ourselves caught up in the 'win-lose' them-against-us mentality of the masculine paradigm, and in the process we've mostly lost trust in the quiet voice of our more-feminine heart and spirit. From our family and culture we've been influenced by spoken or unspoken rules for our gender. Traditionally men have been told to "man up" and women have been told to be seen and not heard. Man-up boys don't cry or they're a sissy – and this has split men off from their feminine side. When we tell our young boys "men don't cry" they must learn to block their emotions, and this creates an imbalance of the masculine and feminine energies in their body and spirit. Meanwhile young girls are taught that their value lies in their appearance and sexuality as seen through the male gaze.

When we look around us at the natural order on our planet, it's obvious that there is an equal amount of dark night and bright day – yin and yang in balance. There's no day without the night. Day represents the masculine energies of action and doing. Night represents the feminine energies of inward qualities such as compassion, reflection, dreaming and restoration. When we disown or cut off one side of ourselves in this regard, imbalance results.

Imagine if there was an imbalance of day and night. Imagine what it would be like if we were never allowed to rest and restore ourselves. We all need daylight and sun and we also need rest and nurturing – a balance of the two opposites. Work and play during one phase ... and rest and sleep during the other. Day gives way to night, they complement each other. Anything in excess is not good for balance. The masculine qualities include logic, individuation, reason, strategic planning, solution-focused action, intellectual strength, the impulse to manipulate and control, to pursue something to a conclusion. Women need these qualities as well as men do. And surely men need the more-feminine qualities including deep honest emotional expression, trusted sparks of intuition, a sense of flowing and participating, plus allowing, accepting, surrendering, trusting and feeling connected – belonging to a greater integrated whole.

Let's be clear – to access and express your feminine side as a male, or your masculine side as a female, doesn't make you any less grounded in your physical gender. And of course, the balance must be found within your particular personality and inclination. Your challenge is to tune into your identity in this regard – and also to notice where you're out of balance. The fact that we have an out-of-balance masculine society based on power, control and competition doesn't mean we must personally stay out of balance.

On so many levels it's through the joining of the sun and the moon, the masculine and feminine in equilibrium, in energetic balance that true transformation is attained. And self-discovery always implies getting to know our own sense of balance in this regard. Feminine wisdom draws on the principles of receptiveness, intuition, emotional intelligence, healthy relationships, and inner stillness. The feminine is receptive and governs *'being'*. The masculine is exertive and governs *'doing'*.

So the question is: When you look deeply to your own inner condition, what do you feel you need more or less of? Not 'what do you *want* more of' but 'what do you *need* more of,' in order to be balanced within your true nature? In what realms of your being do you perhaps need to focus loving attention and alter your male-female stance in life?

And while dealing with this dualistic yin/yang balance, let's always continue to remember the yin-yang unity symbol, where optimally there's a higher sense of unity and oneness surrounding the merger of yin and yang. When we're overly fixated on yang energy we over-value productivity and action, and consider inaction to be a sign of weakness. When we're obsessed with speed and data, when we're caught up in a whirlwind of yang madness and endless busyness, we also are prone to chronic anxiety and stress-related illnesses.

As a culture, we need more time and attention being focused on yin qualities, we need time to do nothing, to rest, to dream, to wonder, to be creative. But of course doing nothing is seen as being lazy. Meditative calm and bliss are not valued at all in most circles. We constantly push our children to never be idle. We deny them the time and space to just play, to goof off and be utterly unproductive! And now we give them smart phones to distract them from their deeper inner experiences.

With all the negativities abounding these days in all our lives, I do want to say that loads of people and organizations are right now doing the good work, actively pushing toward that exquisite balance of these two universal forces. Without hope our entire human culture will crash – so it's wise to focus on the good we see around us, and work to further the light of this universal goodness of spirit. My writing and your reading this book are an organic part of this positive upthrust.

What To Do

Let me share with you the basic guidance I offer my clients in this regard. First of all I make sure they don't think they have to judge themselves negatively in order to begin striving toward their optimum yin/yang balance. The truth is, we can't change ourselves – we can only more-fully discover and manifest who we are. And in the act of self-discovery, in the process of focusing our attention on any imbalances we might find inside us, we'll naturally activate our innate inner process of moving toward equilibrium.

Our entire physical system knows exactly how to maintain equilibrium on so many fronts – we maintain optimum body temperature, our lungs keep us optimally oxygenated, our blood pressure stays relatively even, our heart pumps nutrients to every part of our body – and all this happens without our ego mind doing anything at all. Truly amazing!

And in similar manner, given half a chance, so will your inner sense of self grow and evolve toward optimal balance, depending on your personality and what you're engaged in at the time. We all have situations in our life that demand a strong male presence – and hopefully we all have special moments where a deep feminine sense of surrender, compassion, nurturing and union is needed. To actively attain this flexibility between yin and yang, what can be done?

First of all, we need to create more open space and free time where we can turn our attention directly to this yin/yang theme. We need to explore the various ways outlined in this book to get in touch with our deeper selves, accept, honor and love who we really are – and be open to honoring and releasing all our emotions. And let's shout this loud and clear: if we remain over-busy all the time, we simply won't advance in our desired direction. If we have no time to just ease up and 'be' then we'll get to the end of our lives never having really lived at all. Sure, there will be sunsets and warm hearts and moments of bliss and insight surrounding us. But if we're chronically busy, fixated on doing things all the time, we'll miss out. And that would be a truly sad life. What's the point of spending all your life doing and then you drop dead before you learn how to BE.

Here's a clue to finding inner balance. Feminine energy is *experientially focused,* whereas masculine energy is *results-oriented.* We need both of these energies to survive and thrive. And while yin and yang are opposite of one another, this doesn't mean they are oppositional or in conflict. Instead they complement each other. Think of a battery: there are two sides to a battery, a plus side and a minus side. Both of these opposites are required in order for a flow of energy to occur. Atoms work the same way – balanced opposite charges creating a functional whole.

In this light, as mentioned earlier, all of us have an ego presence that's strongly masculine. It's the 'get things done' in the equation of your life. It's POWER! So what is the equal and opposite of power? Without question it's LOVE. A healthy ego knows to surrender to the power of love quite often – because that's how your organism experiences balance, equilibrium, fulfillment. So you'll want to start observing your daily routines, and see honestly where you're focused on power and manifestation, and where you're focused on love and experience.

Note that power is goal-oriented, it's focused on the future, whereas love is experience-oriented, it's focused purely in the present moment. If you (like most of us) find that you're over-balanced in the future-fixated 'power' direction, then you'll want to begin opening up more time in your life to present-moment opportunities to just be, experience ... enjoy.

In the universally-known Serenity Prayer it's said this way:

God, grant me the serenity to accept
the things I cannot change,
and the courage to change the things I can –
and the wisdom to know the difference.

The Challenge Of Acceptance

Love is an energy, a felt emotion – not an idea or philosophy or achievement. We don't think love, we feel love. It's a flow between two people, and also a flow between our ego self and our deeper unconditional self. And one of the core ingredients in love is what we call total unconditional acceptance. Conditional love isn't really love at all – it's an unspoken deal where someone will give us their love if we behave the way they require us to.

In contrast, unconditional love requires full acceptance of us just as we are. There's no judgment at all. Hopefully most mothers feel this unconditional love for their infant. But it's a challenge for a mother to continue with this unconditional acceptance as the baby becomes a rambunctious toddler and a two-year-old tyrant. A mother who fully accepts her own self will be able to love the child through all its stages of growing up, and then support the child as it becomes an independent adult.

But note the requirement – that the mother also fully accepts and loves herself. If our mother didn't, then we have a challenge to come to love ourselves unconditionally. And if we don't accept ourselves unconditionally, we're not going to be able to love our children unconditionally – unless we act to break the cycle.

And ... we're right back where we started with this book – the fact that a neurotic ego doesn't accept itself unconditionally. So again we must see if this is us – and do something about it if it is. When Jesus said, "Judge not, or you're going to be judged," these words still ring out as an immense challenge. He also said "Fear not," as mentioned earlier. And note that he didn't say 'set a future goal to someday stop judging and being afraid'. He stated this as an actual order – do this now!

In this spirit I urge you to right now decide to stop judging and worrying – not later on in your life. It might sound impossible – but it's your choice, right now. Choose to just go ahead and love yourself just as you are in this moment. Begin practicing unconditional love. All of us are imperfect, we have all sorts of obvious or subtle dents in our personality, we have many reactive programs that might make us a bother at times. But hey, this is who we are ... and right now we need to be loved, not down the road when we become perfect.

You have your ego self and you have your deeper self. The ego judges, the deeper self accepts. So who's going to dominate your life? Perhaps that's your primary choice to make – and then all else shall flow naturally step by step. If you're a practicing Christian, come on – follow the path Jesus clearly laid out for you – stop judging and worrying! And if you're not a practicing Christian, take the advice of one of the deepest spiritual teachers of all time.

What happens when you commit to not judging yourself and others? Every situation you're in, just observe when you're reflexively judging someone – and say to yourself, no, stop the judging. Open your heart to this person, or to yourself, without conditions. Just accept and flow, love and participate. And each time you go through this process, love yourself for taking the challenge.

Judgment is always defensive. We see something that might threaten us at some level, so we judge it and reject it. But we don't have to go through that rejection process in order to deal with the threat. In fact when we put aside the judgment, we can see the situation clearly and act appropriately. That's what's called nonattachment. And by practicing acceptance we can nurture our ability to participate in life. Judgment separates us. Acceptance unites us. It's that simple really. And what makes you feel better, being in isolation or being a participant in a community?

And the same goes for our sense of self-love. If we don't love and accept ourselves just as we are right now, we seriously damage our chances of improving ourselves. It's not really a paradox. If we love ourselves we're going to want to improve ourselves where needed. Love stimulates healing! Rejection provokes more damage. Again – it's your choice. And once you clearly see the options, there's hardly a choice, it is obvious which decision will serve you best.

If you look with love at yourself in terms of the yin/yang balance, you'll realize that too much yin energy will leave you open to becoming aimless to the point of not having a sense of direction, purpose or participation – if you just let it all hang out while life slips you by, that's not optimal. While it's often helpful to be easy-going, too much passivity can turn into being unmotivated, or perhaps a feeling of having little control over your life. Then again, too much yang energy can be equally problematic, you can be unfairly controlling, trying to micromanage all outcomes, and manipulate conditions to your advantage – too much ego-dominance. An egotistic person is always judgmental and therefore not very lovable.

Right now simply ask yourself the question: do you lean more toward the yin energy of soft passivity or the yang energy of hard action? I challenge you to begin cultivating an awareness regarding which energy could best serve you in any given situation. There's no right answer – just your answer.

Take some time to contemplate these elicitor questions:

> *Do you often experience an inability to ease up, relax and let go?*
>
> *Are you habitually a judgmental person?*
>
> *Have you a need for constant stimulation, and maybe can't sit still and just be content with yourself?*
>
> *Do you want to create space in your life for pausing and reflecting before leaping into action?*
>
> *Do you find yourself feeling low on energy to where you just sit around and don't accomplish anything?*
>
> *Do you let people love you just as you are?*
>
> *And who do you accept and love unconditionally?*

Authentic Feminine And Masculine

When we live in our yin we can tap into our innate wisdom, our intuition. We become process-oriented, collaborative. We feel relaxed. Then again as mentioned above, too much yin and we can become sluggish, lazy, overly introverted. We can feel crippled by inaction, and lack any motivation to get things done. Conversely when we live very much in our yang we are ambitious, we accomplish things, we win out over others and succeed because we're so goal-oriented, even to the point of being ruthless. And meanwhile we can't unwind, we might drink too much after work – and our hearts can't soften, play around with the kids, or make love with our partner. Which energy do you habitually spend the most time in?

I've observed in my coaching practice that a lot of working professionals feel depleted in yin energy. Their yang egos are driving them to stay hard and fight – but much of this fighting spirit is actually a sign of weakness because it's fear-driven. I coach these clients in the direction of exploring ways they can begin to slow down, to delegate, to create space in their lives to include self-care practices.

I encourage them to begin to implement a work/life balance, to invite more yin energy and activities and emotions back into their lives. I often do the life-pie exercise with my clients. The areas on the life-pie are: family, work, money, health, relationships, hobbies and spirituality. I get them to look at the pie and think of their life in this regard. Then they can decide for themselves where they want to spend their time in each coming day – and act on that decision.

This can be hard if the ego is always worrying about money and success. And of course this goes for women as well as men. We're all susceptible to going too far into the yang, especially if we're being driven by a neurotic ego. A great many women are over-balanced in the yang direction in our culture – we mistakenly thought that women's lib involved letting women do the traditional work of men. But true liberation is letting both men and women equally participate in the full range of life's activities.

What is lost in a yang-based society? Our female qualities enable us to experience the world through intuition and awareness. We know the importance of the heart. We embody emotional awareness, sensitivity and right-relationship. We're responsible for birth not just physically but also emotionally and spiritually. Yin personifies flowering. The female principle is devoted to the truth. Yin can take all that is troubling, and transform it. Our female principle births the future with ease and grace. Our female presence has the ability to receive thankfully and give without expecting a return. All things grow under her touch. She emanates the essential qualities of love, nurturing, comfort and sanctuary.

Do you feel these yin qualities alive and well within you?

And what are the authentic qualities of masculinity? Yang experiences the world through the intellect and logic. He can be described as the hunter. He has attributes of strength and how-to wisdom. He is the true protector, and will go out of his way to watch over those who need his protection. He is the initiator, the problem-solver. He has a willingness and intent to make things better. He finds the way forward outwardly. He has courage and energy to begin and sustain projects. He is a responsible leader who has vision and wants to find a better way. He is a leader, a scout and an explorer.

Of course we're dealing with stereotypes and archetypes here, but I think you get the idea. And also I think you can see how a balance between the two make us a whole person. Each of us developed certain qualities overmuch, and other qualities undermuch. The imbalance throws off our ability to lead a good life – and so yes, we seek out help as we also try to help ourselves regain our balance.

HE is the archetypal ***HEAD.***

SHE is the archetypal ***HEART.***

Obviously both are essential.

CONCLUSION

"There is a time for everything
and a season for every activity
under the heavens."

Old Testament Saying

We do need to recognize when to act and when to step back, when to pursue relentlessly and when to wait patiently – when to offer to bring the impetus of profound harmony to our daily lives and when to allow things to resolve themselves without interruption. And if we hold the goal of balance always in our minds, even when we temporarily go to extremes we can still swiftly regain equilibrium.

A vital female quality is the ability to sense subtle energetic happenings and flows – and to participate in and guide those that further our life and the health of our community. Being able and willing to sense when yang power is called for, and when yin compassion is best, lies at the heart of wisdom in action.

Do you have this wisdom? Are you open to developing this sensitivity? If so, you're a special person in your community. You can lead when needed – and quietly observe otherwise. And you can help to nurture a balanced sense of male/female energy in both your own heart and the hearts of others.

CHAPTER NINE

Discover Your Vision

~~~~~~~~~~~~~~~~~~~~~~~~

All the greatest and most important problems of life are fundamentally insoluble ... they can never be solved, but only outgrown. This "outgrowth" proves on further investigation to require a new level of consciousness, some higher or wider interest appearing on the horizon – and through this broadening of outlook the insoluble problem loses its urgency. It is not solved logically in its own terms, but fades when confronted with a new and stronger life urge.

Carl Jung

Just when the caterpillar thought the world was over, it unexpectedly became a butterfly.

The metamorphosis from caterpillar into butterfly: during this stage the caterpillar's old body dies and a new body forms inside a protective shell known as a chrysalis. This pupal stage is spent in a chrysalis where the caterpillar's body is broken down and reorganized into the structure of the beautiful butterfly we know and love. Out with the old and in with the new. It is necessary to empty out the old to make room for the new – then life can be full and overflowing. So yes, we all need to release the old so we can embrace the new.

If you want to make a new beginning
throw away your old clothes.

Chinese Proverb
~~~~~~~~~~~~~~~~~~~~~~~~

Years ago I came across the following similar butterfly-rebirth analogy, that of removing old furniture – and the metaphor remains in my mind as a clear path to making real change in one's life. Let's say that I agree to come over to your home, and help you get rid of all your old furniture. It's ragged and has become uncomfortable and just doesn't feel like the real you anymore. A lot of the furniture and fixtures were given to you by your parents – and you know you need a fresh start.

So one day I come over and help you move all your furniture out into your garage once and for all. We remove every piece, every dish, every rug, table, bed, sofa and chair. And we sweep and mop and clean every surface. By evening we're done, and I leave you standing in the middle of your empty spotless house. You look around you and think, "This is great, I've gotten rid of all my old baggage. Now I can look forward to bright new beginnings."

A little later that evening, after spending an hour or two with nothing but yourself and an empty house, what do you suppose you will do? You'll probably get tired of standing, and go out into the garage where the old furniture is stored and get a chair! A little later, you make another trip to the garage and bring in a table, a dish or two, a book and a lamp. You find the emptiness a bother, and you were so comfortable with the things and habits you had lived with in your life thus far. It makes no difference if those things and habits aren't the best for you – it's what you know, it's what you are most secure in keeping at your side.

By nine o'clock you may have retrieved the trusty old TV, and one by one you bring all your old trusted and time-worn stuff back into your house. Soon your desire for change has been overwhelmed by your need for comfort and familiarity.

Why is this regression happening? Because when I helped you remove the old furniture we forgot about finding new furnishings with which to replace the old. The result is quite predictable – when you decided to change your old furnishings (habits and attitudes), but didn't have in hand an immediate new set of furnishings (habits and attitudes) to replace the old, you naturally regressed to the comfortable, old habits of your past. If I were to visit you again in a few weeks you would probably have all your old furnishings back in your house. Perhaps you've rearranged things for a slightly different look, but it would be the same old furniture, the same old programming you had in the first place.

So instead, when we finish emptying your house of the old stuff, you have a shiny new delivery truck full of the most beautiful furniture you've ever imagined. For the next two or three hours we bring in all the beautiful new furniture (new habits) into your (mental) house – and this time we don't store the old furniture in the garage, we load it into a garbage van and send it forever off and away. We get rid of it.

And when you walk back into your house, what was once a place of tattered hopes and broken-down dreams is now filled with your chosen bright new beginnings expressing an exciting new you. And having chosen well, your new mental and emotional furniture stands on the sturdy legs of wisdom and self-assurance. You have replaced frustration, boredom and quiet resignation with the enthusiasm of promise and vision.

This is the difference between just believing in positive thinking and spiritual awakening and actually creating it in your life. It is fine to throw out the ineffective and unfulfilling old patterns and negative energies – that act is essential. But it is also essential to replace the old with the new – a new attitude toward life, a new process for supporting that attitude, and a new vision to guide you and sustain you into your new life.

We are creatures of habit. It's estimated that around 90% of all our rambling thoughts are almost identical to the same ones we ran through our minds the day before. We get up at the same time each morning, run the same worries and plans through our minds, go through the same routine in the bathroom, brush our teeth with the same hand, sit in the same chair and eat the same breakfast. Most of us usually drive the same route or take the same bus or train to the same job, usually thinking and feeling similar thoughts and feelings to the day before – and at the end of the day we drive home, mull over a lot of the same thoughts and emotions, deal with family issues, eat dinner and watch our favorite TV shows. We then go to bed – and without thinking of alternatives we do it all over again the next day.

We do live a big part of our lives running mostly on autopilot. Habitually thinking the same thoughts within the same emotions and attitude structures predictably leads us to the same feelings and behaviors. And thus we unconsciously create the same experience. As a result things stay the same. We have perhaps read in meditation books that change is all there is – but most of us don't like change at all. When we at times step into the river of change it feels uncomfortable and often scary because we're not in charge of the flow and it might sweep us away.

All of this is related directly to our ego's fear of change. Ever since we were four or five, our budding ego has been building an illusory sense of a changeless world, at least a changeless ego and inner personality stance. But now a deeper wisdom inside us, usually the more feminine side of us, is yearning to move beyond the old programs and discover who we really are. And yes, this disturbs and threatens our ego's sense of dominance and importance.

In fact, in the work I do with clients the ego has reason to be afraid of losing its control and fading from importance. Often people can make steps in this expansive direction on their own, or using self-help books and meditation videos and such to guide them. When this doesn't quite do the desired job, then a life coach or therapist can step in and help with the process.

Note that for this all to happen, there must be something within us beyond the ego that is willing to surrender to a higher flow in life. The ego itself can be overly imbalanced in yang directions and fight change – or it can have some deeper nurturing yin aspects that wisely welcome change and even risk transformation.

So in our empty-house metaphor, the proper progression is this. First you feel the impulse for change, for growth, for awakening. Then you consider how to empty your house of the old habits and attitudes. Then you consider what options you have, what direction you want to move in – what vision you have of your optimum future. Then with or without help, you remove the old furnishings. This is sometimes called the death of the ego or its surrender to a higher wise path. Then you immediately bring in the process of establishing new habits, fresh attitudes, and a deeper vision of your future.

Most of us have been conditioned basically from birth to run from and otherwise dodge the unknown. We have to learn ways to become more comfortable in letting go, surrendering to the new – and finding a deeper inner center upon which to build our new life. The unknown is simply that which we have not yet encountered. If for just a few minutes each day we pause, quiet our minds and focus our attention toward the new, we can gently explore what newness might arise – new feelings, new ideas, new hopes and vision.

This is a lifelong process that needs steady exploring and discovery over time. As I see it, there's no ultimate goal here.

A life of self-discovery isn't built on future imaginations and fantasy destinations. Life is an adventure, a journey from birth to death ... and perhaps beyond. The ego runs on future projections and goals. The higher self runs on present-moment experience. The good life is an always-changing flow, not an established unchanging state of chronic stagnation.

For me, our true nature is that of creators both internally and externally. We're continually making choices that determine how we create our lives. And living each new moment as creators is an exciting adventure, it is like living in a different world than the ego's mirage of a changeless life. As soon as we begin to risk welcoming change, each new moment becomes interesting, exciting and special. Why? Because we get involved in and take full responsibility for our lives.

There is always the bright possibility of something new happening. Of course, sometimes change is challenging, threatening, even downright disturbing. But as we've seen, even what we consider negative developments almost always have a silver lining if we stay with our feelings of uncertainty long enough to see what opportunities are presenting themselves to us. Again – in any situation, if we keep our ego calm and our hearts open, going ahead and flowing with the change at hand will usually present us with something valuable, important – and ultimately fulfilling.

And I might mention, related to our house-cleaning analogy – you don't have to throw the baby out with the bathwater. In fact it's always wise to honor and carry forward the valuables from the past ... the enduring wisdom, the deeper traditions that have supported communities and civilizations over the ages. What needs discarding is all the rubbish the ego accumulates and clings to for stability and control. Anything that rings true, that has beauty, that is grounded in wisdom and love needs to be allowed to stay in your house. Whatever is willing and eager to go with the flow of your new life can surely continue to enjoy a place of reverence in your heart and soul.

Welcoming A New Vision

Unfortunately most people do not spend their lives doing what they love. They don't even have a hopeful vision for their life. Someone once said that a lot of people have a bigger TV screen than they do a vision for their life. They seem more interested in vicariously living off of other people's talents by watching them on television. Millions of people live their whole lives without taking a creative leap and into expressing their deeper selves through singing, dancing, painting, cooking, risking a new business venture, taking adventure trips, exploring inner realms through meditation, and so forth.

It's so much easier and risk-adverse to settle for what was handed to us by our family and situation in life. And anxiety of any kind clearly inhibits creative expression and exploration. If we don't have parents who take leaps, we don't have a role model for doing so ourselves. We can get so used to living our life in a certain way that we fail to even consider developing a vision for how our lives could unfold in new directions. We can continue to run on default attitudes and cautious worldviews and never even get a taste for a life that feels free to explore a new vision of future possibilities.

Please pause and answer this question:

What is your primary goal
at this moment in your life?

If you can't answer that question right away then you are probably not clear regarding your higher passion in life. You might very well be just drifting along in existing family and work ruts, allowing the events and circumstances around you to be the driving force in your life. You might see yourself as 'poor me' and an innocent victim – but nothing could be further from the truth. As we've been seeing in this book, no one but you is determining the myriad of choices that you make day in and day out. If you make just a slight change in your routine or attitude, and then make another, and another, your life does change!

What is needed in order to make decisions that take you into new realms is the desire to manifest a vision that is unique to you, that you have created, that points your attention where your passion wants to flow. And a vision is always creative – it's your imagination conjuring up a new life experience that enables you to blossom rather than wither. Working to manifest your vision will bring you a new sense of purpose and dignity. Your vision of the future will empower you to blossom into your fullness of life.

When you look deeply and begin to sense your true calling in life, you'll also find that an almost magical sense of being guided and supported begins to emerge. New energies rise up from your depths and enable you to take on challenges and move through them successfully. You shift from worrying about doing something to having the courage to do that thing! But this won't happen until you reflect, meditate, dream, imagine, research and otherwise focus your attention precisely on this question of what you're really here to accomplish in this lifetime.

There's a parable in the Bible where Jesus curses a fig tree because it hasn't blossomed. The message is clear – bloom or be pruned. In the Gospel of Thomas, Jesus is quoted as saying:

If you bring forth what is within you,
what you bring forth will save you.

If you do not bring forth what is within you,
what you do not bring forth will destroy you.

Those are very strong words. And note that Jesus isn't saying we must bring forth a particular thing or talent. All he's saying is that whatever is within us, we need to bring it forth and not leave it stuck inside us. This applies directly to what we're talking about in this book. What's within us includes both our wounds and our gifts. If we don't bring our wounds forth into the light of awareness, they will quite realistically, in psychological and spiritual terms, destroy us. If we release our inner pain and anxiety, this will save us from chronic emotional suffering.

And equally, if we bury our talents and aspirations, that inhibition can also on subtle levels damage our lives and destroy a potential future. There's another parable in the New Testament where Jesus admonishes people for hiding their lamp away rather than bringing their light (their talent) forth into the community. Consider your own talents – have you identified what you're really good at and love to do? And have you yet brought it forth?

If not, what you need is a vision, a plan, a sense of determination and commitment to manifesting your vision. This doesn't mean you necessarily need to drop everything and fly to Nepal to climb the mountain. It means you need to have a vision for the general direction you want to move in – and take the first baby steps in that direction ... and then see what next step naturally emerges. Setting a final goal is not as important as feeling moved to take that first step that feels good to you.

If you don't have a hope and a design and a plan for your life, chances are you'll fall into someone else's plan. Having a vision is what makes life more exciting and worthwhile. Without a vision, it's is too easy to get side-tracked. It's so easy to wander and drift through life accomplishing very little that you feel good about.

Riding The Life Force

People with a vision have no time for drama. They also have no time to dwell in anxiety and depression. Instead they invest their time and energy into being creative on their chosen path. And here's another important thing about having a vision – it will give you the vitality that makes you feel alive and eager to get up in the morning. Having a vision will inspire you to focus on what really matters to you. And as you focus your power of attention each new day toward manifesting your vision, you'll do just that.

All of us do naturally possess a still-mysterious life force that moves us forward. Most little kids are strongly in touch with this invisible flow of vitality and adventure, enthusiasm and discovery. An old Taj Mahal (the blues singer, not the temple) song put it this way:

Remember the feeling as a child
when you woke up and the morning smiled.
It's time to feel like that again!

This universal source of creativity and energy is always available for expression through each of us. As I said before, existence itself needs us to participate in the unfolding of this present moment. We are all part of an infinite integrated whole. Our individual heartbeat is part of the universal pulse of life on this planet. Our ongoing challenge is to relearn how to participate more fully in the universal dance.

And always remember – you are unique, your character traits are a biochemical neurocognitive DNA mix that will never be repeated. There are ideas unique to you, a specific rhythm and perspective and trajectory that are your strengths. You are here for a reason, you have your special impact to make, no matter how subtle.

Ask these questions of yourself:

What was I brought into existence to accomplish?

What situations most energize me?

What am I most passionate about?

In what ways do I see myself as a hero?

Deep inside my hopeful heart, what springs to mind
as a new vision for my optimum future?

But here's the reality-orient: simply wishing for success to come into your life isn't enough. You need to nurture a vision and then each day act on it! Your vision will provide you with a sense of direction and enduring hope – an authentic reason for living. If you feel content, great. But if not, don't spend your life slaving away doing work you don't like with people you don't resonate with.

One vision I had years ago was to break free from working nine to five on a daily basis. My vision was to only do work I love and to have a work-life balance. Another vision for me was to write and publish my own book. And look! Like a Disney character once sang in a movie:

You gotta have a dream!
If you don't have a dream,
how you gonna have a dream come true?

So what are you gonna do with your precious life? I recommend waking up each morning and asking yourself that core question. Like I said, if you're already feeling fulfilled, your morning thought might simply be how thankful you are that you were able to fulfill your vision. And if you have habits that you love, definitely enjoy them! However, I suspect that even if you feel you've succeeded with past visions, most of us will have multiple visions throughout our lives, as our situations and intentions and involvements evolve. Our main driving vision might be to find work we love, to find a wonderful life partner – and then perhaps creating and raising and then sending out into the world our children.

Perhaps what's most important to us is our managing to live with fresh clean air and quiet nearby woods and a warm hearth and supporting community. Equally you might strive to help guide your community or business in a more empathic and sustainable direction. I'm in no way saying a vision has to be earth-shaking or even noticed by the rest of the world. It's your vision ... and it optimally emerges not from your ego mind but from your responsive heart, from your gut instinct, and hopefully from your deeper spiritual sense of your unique life calling.

As a beginning, you might start to identify what matters most to you in your life. Of course there might be millions of people on this planet who have similar passions and goals. Others will also be blessed with a parallel vision. At heart human beings share a whole host of related needs and intentions. Just take a look at your own life – are you living each day on your own terms, or still confined by what your parents and peers and community expect of you? Ultimately you'll want to move beyond using the word 'should' in your vocabulary. Your life vision needs to be uniquely yours, which means you need to find it for yourself.

I recommend making your vision far-reaching, requiring a stretch to accomplish. Your vision is best seen as an on-going dream that you are striving to move fully into.

So each new day, return your focus to what works for you and what gives you pleasure – and de-prioritize everything else. The trick is to not let yourself be conned by your own ego or the influence of others into being driven by obligations and activities that don't honor or serve you. Nurture your vision, choose a long-term focus and commitment, have an ever-evolving plan of action – and stay the course until you begin to get results. A vision without a plan is a fantasy. A vision with a plan is a happening.

Gently over time, develop your vision of the day-to-day life you want to manifest, the things you truly want, the household ambiance that will nurture your inner growth, the job that resonates with your personal intentions, the relationships that sustain you emotionally, the quality of each new day you would like to enjoy – what in fact is your ideal day, week, month, year? Do you want to spend the rest of your life dreading that Monday feeling, or do you want to create the life your spirit and soul really yearn for?

To achieve your goals, you must learn to have a mind of your own. Find out through inner inquiry and discovery what makes you most happy, what brings you true joy in life – and then act on this by actually doing those very things! This is your life, and this is not a dress rehearsal. Are you living the life of your own choosing? Are you doing what you truly desire with your unique talents? Or are you just going along with what is expected of you, day in and day out? Are you just following the crowd, caught up in roles and duties and obligations? Are you still living the script set by your parents and community – or have you put a new show on the road?

Billy Joel sings a song called *My Life* which goes like this:

I don't care what they say anymore –
this is my life.

Go ahead with your own life.
Leave me alone.

Creativity is all about self-expression. It's an outflow of your essence, it's your gift to the world. In all cultures, it's been observed since the beginning of history that what makes us feel best is being of service in our community. So let's not cheat our neighbors of our contribution to society's higher good. And equally, let's learn how to thankfully receive the contributions from others. Again – balance is all. And our external balance begins with internal balance:

If you want to be acknowledged, acknowledge yourself.

If you want to be valued, value yourself.

If you want to be accepted, accept yourself.

If you want to be seen, see yourself.

If you want to be heard, listen to yourself.

If you want to feel loved – love yourself!

Whatever you want from other people, you can learn to give it to yourself. Be your own advocate in your own life. Learn to nurture a mind of your own. Really, what does make you feel happy, what brings you joy in life? Determine that – and then right now start doing those things. If you are constantly yearning, complaining, dreaming and pining, then this 'poor me' weak broadcast is what you're sending out, and how people will see you, and what you'll manifest. Instead, be thankful for everything you do have – rejoice in all your good fortune – no bombs dropping on your head, no food shortages, only occasional weather disasters, and at least a somewhat-free society to move around in. And most importantly, you have a mind and a heart and a soul that you can use to help make this an even better world for future generations. Protect, regularly honor and fully appreciate what you do have!

When we focus chronically on what we don't have rather than focusing on what we do have, we fill our hearts and minds with a debilitating sense of lack. Remember the Mexican fisherman. He expressed the wisdom of simplicity. Bring into your life experiences and relationships that sustain your soul, rather than fixating on physical things that in themselves don't bring happiness and fulfillment. Instead they can cause all sorts of complications and obligations that tie us down rather than set us free.

We are far more powerful in the creation of our lives than we realize. To paraphrase Gandhi: we need to become the change we wish to see in the world. If we don't choose how we live with conscious intention, we will live it by default, following along after others. We don't have to be important or special or famous – all we actually need is reasonable sustainable success and authentic pleasure in whatever it is that we choose to do.

Values Matter

Answer this question right now:

What is your number one core value for your life?

If you can't answer this question, perhaps you have never given much thought to what your core values and primary virtues are. With clients I often have them reflect on and identify their top five core values. Then in the spirit of self-discovery I have them look deeply to see if their lives are aligned and congruent with their core values. You might want to do this yourself as a basic insight adventure.

Understanding your values will help you recognize areas of your life that need more of your daily attention. Your values and the virtues you aspire toward define what is most meaningful to you. As you learn to stay attuned to your underlying values, they will guide each of your choices in life. For example, someone who values family might try to spend extra time at home, while someone who values success in their career may do just that opposite.

My number-one core value in life has always been freedom. Our whole world civilization is continually choosing either to sink into an authoritarian rule or a government dedicated to maximizing individual freedom. Do we want to be mature adults and take responsibility for nurturing the higher good – or do we want to regress back to when our lives were ruled by adults who gave us really very little freedom?

So again – what do you most value in your life? It seems that a great many people don't know how important an awareness of one's personal values is. The Christian religion like most other religions has a set list of virtues we're supposed to try to live by – but these are mere lists. I encourage you to put aside such theological approaches to virtues and values, and find your own words for what matters most to you. The list can be short or long – just write down what comes to mind, rank-order them in light of primary importance – and right now today, commit to nurturing these qualities in your own life.

What must you have in life to experience fulfillment?

What values are ESSENTIAL to your life?

What virtues represent your PRIMARY WAY OF BEING?

Once you begin to clarify what values drive you, and see clearly which virtues define your sense of the good life, a next essential step in envisioning your future is to do just that – set your mind and heart and imagination free to explore not just your regular known world of possibilities, but also to envision beyond your current circumstances. A vision is a dream of possibility that knows no limits. So use your vision quest to dream beyond what your eyes can see – and then do the work to make your dream become a reality. Let your vision for your life be defined not by what you see, but by how vividly you can dream.

One of my favorite films is *Shirley Valentine*. In the film Shirley wonders as an adult how she lost the girl she once was. Throughout the film we get glimpses of the great humor and quick wit which Shirley possessed in her youth. Then we see with the passing of time how the person she was just drifted away. Her marriage is now in the dead zone, full of roles, duties and boring routines. In frustration, Shirley decides to go on a solo vacation to Greece, where she begins to rediscover herself – and regains her own unique spark. She gets in touch with her vision again!

This film shows that no matter what the past has been, we can begin anew – and have a fresh start no matter what stage of life we find ourselves in. We are all busy writing the story of our life. If we are honest with ourselves, we all have an urge to feel that we've done something worthwhile with our lives – that we haven't squandered our time here on Earth. I'm writing this book and doing my life coaching in this spirit – that no matter where we currently find ourselves, we can take responsibility for how we run our minds, tune in more deeply to our heart and gut impulses and wisdom ... and truly discover and manifest our life purpose.

CONCLUSION

There are lots of great books written on the manifestation process and the creative process. One of my favorite books is

The Path of Least Resistance by Robert Fritz. I did a three-month course with him and his son Ivan, on *Creating*. Robert explains the creative process in great detail – and his summation was that we're all born to create, and that as the metaphor says, we don't want to die with our music still locked up in us.

Kahlil Gibran said:

When you are born
your work is placed in your heart.

Why are we so moved when we go to the theatre and see an amazing performance, or go to a concert and are deeply touched by the music? It's because of the vibrant flow of creativity coming from these performers that touch our hearts and souls. We find ourselves resonating with the emotions being expressed. We feel part of a larger human whole. It's the same when we pause for just a few breaths outside, feel sunlight on our skin, and hear the tiny song of a bird nearby. We temporarily let go of our habitual sense of ego isolation, and instead allow our own hearts to sing, to participate in the cacophony of life.

In my coaching business I love the fact that I get the opportunity to empower people to realize their life vision. It's such a rewarding career. And however you choose, I strongly encourage you to be the creative force in your own life. Discover what really matters to you and then go do it. The poet T.S. Eliot warned that if we are unwilling to establish and live by our own terms for our life, we must helplessly accept the terms life imposes on us. So … let's set our own terms.

CHAPTER TEN

The Fine Art Of Forgiveness

~~~~~~~~~~~~~~~~~~~~~~~~~~~~~~~

He who is devoid of the power to forgive
is devoid of the power to love.
There is some good in the worst of us
and some evil in the best of us.
When we discover this we are
less prone to hate our enemies.

Martin Luther King Jr

Forgiveness is the key to peace. It is the greatest healer of all. Forgiveness frees the soul. Ask yourself: do you want to be free? Forgiveness benefits you and the person you're forgiving – so do it for both of you. And of course let's learn to regularly pause and forgive ourselves. That's where forgiveness begins.

Real forgiveness is a strength. Gandhi said: *"The weak can never forgive. Forgiveness is the attribute of the strong."* The golden rule states that you do unto others as you would have them do unto you. What you wish upon others you wish upon yourself. In this sense as in so many others, we're all part of a larger whole. Who knows – perhaps we can even manage to forgive humankind for not always being so kind.

This concept of forgiveness has appeared in Buddhism, Christianity, Hinduism, Islam, Judaism, Taoism and almost all of the world's religions. There are many reasons why it's best to forgive. It may seem unnatural or selfish to admit that forgiving someone is an act you do for yourself, not the other
~~~~~~~~~~~~~~~~~~~~~~~~~~~~~~~

person. It frees you from an otherwise-negative inner feeling of judgment. Forgiveness by the way doesn't condone that other person's actions, it doesn't mean what happened was okay and it certainly doesn't mean that person is still welcome in your life. Forgiveness means you have made peace with the pain and hurt of a past transgression – and are ready to let your negative emotions related to that transgression (or perceived transgression) go and be gone.

The process is to acknowledge the good and the bad from your time together with someone, to see that it all served an important purpose in both your lives ... and then to de-charge the memory and move on free of it all. This is an inner healing process, a spring-cleaning of the mind and heart. It clears up inner space for new experience that's free from the weight of the past.

Not forgiving keeps us trapped in resentment and bitterness. The opposite of forgiveness is stagnation, which prohibits further growth and new discovery. The choice is always: dwell chronically on what someone did and wallow around in upsetting thoughts and feelings – or choose to heal the hurt and set yourself free to move on. And by the way, forgiveness is not at all dependent on the other person. The only person in control of your thoughts and feelings is you. No one can make you forgive them, nor can they stop you from forgiving them.

Many times our inability to forgive others can stem from an inability to forgive ourselves. I encourage my clients to begin to be more tolerant of their own failings, their misdeeds and deeds not done. Let's all acknowledge that to be human is to be imperfect. When we develop compassion for ourselves just as we are, and forgive ourselves, we're then more able to feel compassion for others.

I see forgiveness as a loving gift we give to ourselves. When we hold onto a resentment or a grievance, our body and mind suffer. Here's a transcultural insight: the Aramaic word for 'to forgive' is equal to the English word 'to untie'. Untie yourself from the bindings of resentment and you release yourself from the control the offender has over you.

Always forgive your enemies.
Nothing annoys them so much.

Oscar Wilde

Forgiveness sets you the victim free, and it also liberates the offender. It helps you move forward with your life. It removes the anger from your heart and helps you gain peace of mind. Forgiveness is the best revenge because if you are still holding on then they win. Unresolved conflict can go deeper than you may realize. It may be affecting your physical and mental and even your spiritual wellbeing.

Forgiveness doesn't just happen on its own – it's usually an active process in which you make a conscious decision to let go of the resentment and negative feelings, whether the person deserves this act of grace or not. Your part is to stop judging and start focusing on brighter inner fixations. Very often your offender doesn't even think they did something wrong – and perhaps they didn't from their perspective. That's exactly where long-lasting bitterness and conflict get stuck, even for generations in such situations as clan battles. You can be the peacemaker in this regard. You can make the first step in reconciliation, or at least disengagement from the conflict.

When Jesus is quoted from the New Testament with words encouraging us to love our enemies and to 'turn the other cheek' rather than hitting back, I think most people say "Oh sure," and just toss that compassionate non-violent commandment to the side. How can we take that dangerous piece of advice seriously in our life? But in so many cases we can follow what we discussed earlier, and just not react to things people say to us that are unkind or cutting or downright mean. We can receive the stimulus, note how it pushes our reaction buttons – and instead, breathe evenly, and simply not engage.

At times we definitely need to defend ourselves from outright attacks. But otherwise we can change the entire tone of an encounter by not reacting – by turning the other cheek. Of course, it's often wise to side-step and duck! But notice that when you don't react to an attack, you provide your attacker with a moment to perhaps have their own realization ... and perhaps to pop out of their habitual attack mode.

Some people are more forgiving by nature, and consequently they tend to be more satisfied and content and bright in their lives. People who hang on to grudges are more likely to experience negative health conditions, feel lonely, fail in business and relationships alike. They most likely inherited grudge-holding emotions from their parents and extended family. And they almost always are fixated on ego-based attitudes that have taken over their heart and soul and left them shriveled inside. When you realize this, then compassion for them can arise, and forgiveness has room to rise up and happen ... and heal the conflict.

The Plague Of Resentment

Louise Hay in her book *Heal Your Body* talks about becoming aware that cancer very often comes from a pattern of deep resentment that is held for a long time until it literally eats away at the body. When Louise got vaginal cancer, she began to work with a therapist to clear old patterns of resentment.

She says that up to that time she had not acknowledged that she harbored so much deep resentment. It's all too true that we can be blind to our own negative patterns – but the body never lies, the body keeps the score.

Before Louise became aware of her medical condition, she already had sensed that she needed to do forgiveness work. She'd done some deep releasing and forgiving sessions. But she hadn't really gotten down to the core thought patterns that cause the most dis-ease in the body – self-criticism, anger, resentment and guilt.

What about you – how do you stand in regard to each of these dis-ease causing emotions? Take a deep breath and see how you respond to these questions:

Am I still hanging on to an old hurt?

Is my heart feeling hardened to someone?

Am I often caught up in angry feelings?

Is there someone I really need to forgive?

Can I forgive myself?

In her book, Louise points to mental causes for physical illness, and then offers a metaphysical way to overcome those mental causes. She explores in depth a simple yet profound method that can help to heal your body. And specifically related to this present chapter's theme, in a book called *A Course in Miracles* it's said that all dis-ease comes from a state of un-forgiveness – and whenever we fall ill, we immediately need to look around to see who it is that we need to forgive.

In the case of Louise, she says she was sexually abused as a child. As an adult she realized she had to clear the festering patterns of resentment she'd been holding since childhood. She was literally being eaten alive with cancerous growths because she had not yet forgiven her abuser. Often we can on our own learn to forgive and forget – but with extreme trauma, often professional help is needed. With the help of a good therapist Louise was able to contact and express all the old, bottled-up fear, anger and resentment she'd been carrying around unconsciously for so many years.

And with the emotional and spiritual healing through the power of forgiveness, she recovered from her physical illness. As it says in *The Course in Miracles*, forgiveness is the answer to almost everything. This doesn't mean that we must turn our backs on medical procedures when needed – it just means that there's a deeper emotional and existential subterfuge happening in many medical illnesses that also needs full consideration.

I think the whole concept of forgiveness is too often misunderstood. It simply means choosing to release and let go of your anger, hurt and desire for revenge. Always keep in mind that forgiveness benefits YOU most of all. Holding onto resentment makes it hard or impossible for you to discover your deeper self and experience peace, health and fulfillment. Right now you have the choice to relax in your heart, bring to mind someone you're at odds with, and say to them: "I let go, I accept what happened, I forgive us both." And remember that you can forgive someone without resuming contact or continuing in a relationship with them. You're just permanently disconnecting the reactive feelings in your heart toward them.

Forgiveness cannot be forced, and you may never understand why someone did what they did to you or someone you love. Just break the energetic chain. People who have been hurt too often go on to hurt others – so in a very real way it's your responsibility to forgive, so that you don't broadcast your charge of resentment onto other people. Sometimes you can do this on your own, sometimes it requires you to work through your feelings with a professional guide in order to release all the anger, hurt, pain, etc. Then when you feel ready to move on into forgiving them and setting yourself free, you'll be prepared for the leap.

Sometimes I get my clients who are working toward forgiveness to write a letter that they won't send to the person they are trying to forgive. Writing an uncensored letter is a great way to let it all pour out onto the pages – just consciously acknowledge all the inner feelings that come up as a result of writing the letter. As you bring your pent-up emotions out into the open through the letter, a definite healing takes place through that 'revealing' process. In fact whenever you feel buried emotions under pressure inside you, polluting your thoughts and actions, this method of writing down what you're feeling is an excellent thing to do.

And whenever your life feels stuck, pause, tune into your breathing and your heart – and ask yourself without forethought the question: *Who is it that I need to forgive?* It could be a political group, men in general, women in general, a church or community organization, the human species, even God.

Some people go around for many years, even all their life, harboring the hostile feeling that they have a right to be angry, hurt, depressed, sad and resentful because of what happened to them at some stage of their life. They are certain they're in the right and others are dead wrong. If this is something you struggle with, the question to ask yourself is:

Do you want to be right ... or do you want to be happy?

In the book *The Four Agreements* by Don Miguel Ruiz, the second agreement is: *Don't take anything personally.* In a certain sense, as we discussed before, nothing negative that other people do is because of you – it is because of themselves. You aren't responsible for the actions of others, you are only responsible for your own. When you truly understand this concept, you refuse to take things personally that people try to lay on you through anger and judgment. If someone comes at you with anger and you react with anger, you end up in a fight. If someone comes at you in anger and you don't react, you create the possibility of reconciliation.

Again – forgiveness does not mean you must be a walk-over or a doormat for anyone. If someone treats you poorly, you have within your power the ability to set clear boundaries. And often your best response to hostility is simply to back away until the distance is great enough to dissipate the charge. This is obvious in a bar where a drunk is aggressive – just back away, don't engage – and it works equally well in a work or family conflict. Back off – let the other person deal with their feelings without aiming them at you.

Let's say I make an appointment to see someone next Tuesday at 2 p.m. They don't show up. Later on they call me and give me an excuse as to why they couldn't make it. We re-arrange for the following Tuesday at 2 p.m. and again they don't show up. They call and give me an excuse as to why they couldn't make it again this week. I have information now that this person doesn't keep their commitments, so I refrain from making a third appointment with them. I set my boundary so I won't get disappointed a third time. If someone is doing the same behavior over and over, you need to ask yourself the question: *Why am I allowing this to continue*?

Forgiveness usually requires action. Forgiving someone over and over for the same offence is not enough – learn to change your behavior so that you're not still playing into their pattern. Don't lay blame and try to change their behavior – just forgive, let go, act where needed without laying blame. Removing blame means never assigning responsibility to anyone else for what you're experiencing. When you don't blame you stay in your own power. Not choosing to get offended is really saying I have control over how I'm going to feel. The fool stands and fights – the sage walks calmly away. If someone is unreliable, rude, arrogant, inconsiderate, foolish or stupid, it just gives you information about that person. Become an observer.

Ross Rosenberg coined the saying:

OBSERVE – DON'T ABSORB

Another powerful approach to this is to work at what you are FOR rather than what you are AGAINST. When Mother Theresa was asked to march against the Vietnam War she replied: "No I won't, but when you have a march FOR peace I will be there." Whenever we say we can't forgive someone, we end up expending valuable energy being AGAINST someone or something, rather than using that same energy being FOR yourself and causes you deem just and uplifting.

At the root of most spiritual practices is the notion of actively practicing forgiveness – of actively disengaging from all accusations of blame and guilt for past offences against you. Think of (or write down) every person who has harmed you, cheated you, stole from you, said awful things about you, told lies about you, and so forth. All of that entanglement with negative past experiences is being perpetuated by thoughts that you allow to dominate your consciousness – and that's definitely a heavy burden.

At any moment you can just as easily drop that accusatory charge inside you, so you can regain peace in your heart and mind. And again – when you practice forgiveness you make the conscious (and wise) choice to no longer be in a negative state of hostility with that person. When the situation is looked at dispassionately, the choice will almost always be the same: free yourself from being sapped by the self-defeating energy of resentment.

Resentment is like poison that continues to seep through your system. I love this quote:

If you're going to pursue revenge
you'd better dig two graves.

Chinese Proverb

Getting Even

The well-known author and teacher Wayne Dwyer once said that it was a single act of profound forgiveness toward his father that turned his entire life around – from one of ordinary awareness to one of higher consciousness, more rewarding achievement, and success. I've observed this same healing and recovery of one's potential life force in so many clients over the years.

Vengeance seems to be rooted in the faulty belief that we can be happy only by getting back at someone. Too often this destructive attitude is learned from parents and siblings and peer groups during childhood, and then unfortunately carried over into adulthood. If you think of all the movies you've watched, you'll note that getting revenge is a primary motivation in the story. Motivation in a plot always springs from some emotional need, such as the need for love, power, fame, respect and recognition – or revenge.

Revenge usually generates the most violent action. And that action is based on a primary judgment of violation and guilt. "I must avenge my brother's murder" expresses our cultural tradition that it's our duty to avenge the violation of a relative. The Old Testament spoke of "an eye for an eye" but Jesus spoke of "turning the other cheek."

History has clearly shown that going to war big or small almost never ends in happiness. If we judge someone or a group or a clan or a nation as the cause of our suffering, and then work to make them suffer as much or more than we have, will we in the end be happy – will we then get rid of our pain? When we live lives motivated by vengeance, this will always lead to following a painful destructive path. Living within our own revenge conspiracy constantly aggravates an old wound, and so we reactively keep wounding someone in return – either by actively attacking someone, or withdrawing our attention, love, support and acceptance.

Deep down, too often we perpetuate this consuming mindset of revenge in order to avoid dealing with ourselves rather than blaming the outside world for our suffering. The Fighter is the shadow figure who always wants to settle an issue by force. Fighting implies that we haven't yet reached a level of maturity in which we can feel and express our honest emotions without reacting or laying blame. We're still caught up in a vicious circle of judgment, pain and attack. We're still making others responsible for our experience rather than taking full responsibility for our own inner thoughts and feelings.

Henry Wadsworth Longfellow talked about forgiveness with these words:

If we could read the secret history of our enemies
we should find in each one's life
sorrow and suffering enough
to disarm all our hostility.

What we don't heal we pass on. By seeing another's hostile behavior as a call for help, we can respond with understanding if not compassion – and allow our non-aggressive behavior to open up space for an easing of the tensions. Forgiving is in fact a form of surrender. When we let go of something it often means that something new and truer can fill that place. New possibilities open up when forgiveness appears and new directions can transform the situation. Fresh hope is born of reconciliation.

Webster's dictionary says that forgiveness is the process of giving up the desire to punish. As I mentioned before, with forgiveness the only one involved in the act is the forgiver. I have forgiven loads of people who were not even aware that I had forgiven them. I forgave them for my own peace of mind. If my forgiveness helps them, good – but it's not my primary motivation. My motivation is first of all the impulse to love myself.

Note that we all sometimes talk about "having a grievance against" someone. Revenge is in fact caught up in the grieving process. Elizabeth Kubler Ross talked about the five stages of grieving after suffering a loss: denial, anger, bargaining, depression and acceptance. When someone violates us, almost always they've taken away something we're strongly attached to and fear we can't live without – so naturally we react with anger! But we're supposed to continue through the grieving process, not get stuck long-term in #2. We're supposed to move through the progression of emotions and end up feeling acceptance if we're to heal our trauma and move beyond our sense of loss.

Think of someone you haven't forgiven for something they did to you or your loved ones – and see if you got stuck in the second deadly stage of grieving. In your past someone did or didn't do something to you. At first you might not even believe they did it (denial). Then you get mad at them for doing or not doing it (anger/revenge). Remember that this anger is a natural feeling so don't try to block it. Instead, let that wild energy flood your body – but also allow that emotion to then flow into the unavoidable feeling of depression at your loss.

Only when all these feelings are accepted and moved naturally through, can we arrive on the other side of grieving. If we refuse to flow with our feelings, we end up stuck in either anger or depression – and neither of those in themselves will heal our hearts and let us move forward.

Sometimes I talk about the fact that revenge is always stuck in the past. It's perpetually unfinished business weighing us down – as if we have one foot nailed to the floor and the other trying to move us into the present moment where we can feel alive and able to envision our future. With that nail in our foot we're in constant pain. The only solution is to dive deep emotionally, see how we're being tied to the past by that nail of revenge – and pull that nail out!

Forgiveness always involves release. We must re-experience all the pent-up anger and rage ... and then dive down into the buried emotions of loss, fear, hopelessness, loneliness and whatever else underlies the revenge impulse. Anger they say is a cover-up emotion, a secondary emotion. It's a defense or armor we put up to avoid the underlying hurt, fear or grief that threatens to overwhelm us.

This is an understandable reaction – our ego too often misperceives a danger or threat as life-threatening when it's actually only ego-threatening. As we develop wisdom about life, we can see more and more clearly how we over-react way too often. We often take offence at every little slight, and 'resentment builds up' inside us – but what are we to do, be in forgiveness mode all the time?

Well, if we look to our deep spiritual teachers for guidance, Matthew 18:21-22 says it this way:

Then Peter came up and said to him, "Lord, how often will my brother sin against me and I forgive him? As many as seven times?" Jesus said back to him, "I do not say to you seven times, but seventy-seven times."

What Jesus means is that we need to nurture inside us a constantly-forgiving heart. Get in the habit of forgiving. Let it become second nature because it will set you free. In the parable of the unmerciful servant (Matthew 18:32-33), Jesus paints the picture of a wealthy master who was moved to compassion for a servant who could not pay a substantial debt. Instead of throwing the servant in prison, the master mercifully forgives his servant's debt and sends him on his way.

Forgiveness And Love

To forgive is to know love, which we all say we want more of. But the opposite – holding a grudge – is so common-place that we do it unconsciously. We imagine getting even for the smallest of things. Many of us spend decades resenting another's behavior. Maybe a spouse had an affair, a sibling took advantage of us, a teacher never favored us at school, or a parent unfairly punished us. Let's just hold in mind that whatever happened yesterday or last year or twenty years ago can be forgiven.

I think we all agree that being revengeful very often generates inner stress and fatigue, confusion and imbalance. We've all experienced the relief that comes from patching things up with a co-worker or spouse or sibling. Let's put a sign up on our wall: *Forgiveness Heals*. Every act of conflict moves us further away from inner peace. Few people would claim to want turmoil or stress or war in their lives. But we go around wishing bad luck on the people who hurt us, waiting for the day when they get their comeuppance. Out of unconscious habit and cultural training we wish ill to befall our enemies – and nation to nation this revengeful posture can continue even though no one at all benefits.

It is never wise to seek or wish
for another's misfortune.
If malice or envy were tangible
and had a shape
it would be the shape
of a boomerang.

Charley Reese

In the Christian tradition, one of the last things Jesus said as he hung on the cross looking out over the crowd jeering for his murder was a message of love, truth ... and forgiveness:

Father forgive them
for they know not what they do.

I was trained in the NVR (non-violent resistance) model which was developed by Haim Omer and a team working with him at the University of Tel Aviv in Israel. The main characteristic of this non-violent approach to conflict was first of all to decide to be brave and stand up to ongoing oppression – and then to commit to a nonviolent approach, even when the other side takes violent measures. Jesus, Buddha, Gandhi, Martin Luther King Jr and Nelson Mandela all taught a similar approach to autocracy and dictatorship. Non-violence is the active, purposeful pursuit of peace.

Rather than pointing blame and hungering for revenge for past deeds, NVR developed a particular approach (called non-violent communication or NVC) to resolve conflict in communities or families that are being torn apart by internal discord. Everyone caught up in the conflict is welcomed into an NVC gathering, and each person is allowed to fully speak their peace without any interruption and with everyone else respectfully listening. Once a grievance is fully expressed by one person, then the next gets to hold the talking stick and speak out their grievance – and state their unmet need clearly.

As the stick goes round the circle of leaders of opposing sides of a conflict, almost a miracle often happens. By the end of a session the deeper unmet needs of all sides have been fully aired and honored – and in this process, by coming to appreciate all sides and all needs equally, the circle can come to a greater shared understanding of why everyone has their grievances. And in this new shared state of understanding, compromises and resolutions are expressed and agreed to by all parties. In fact a rule of NVC is that everyone stays in the circle until resolution is achieved.

Another parallel method I've studied is called *Ho'oponopono*. It's the ancient Hawaiian ritual of forgiveness. It comes from the Hawaiian understanding of the unity of everything in the world, where even though we feel ourselves to be separate, the universe is one song. Uni-verse. Ho'oponopono is a powerful way for a community in conflict to come together and hear all sides of a conflict, and then as a unified group to seek an agreement that serves the whole community, and re-establishes a shared approach for working together in cooperation and peace.

Asking To Be Forgiven

The Hawaiians call their group of islands 'The Land of Aloha' or the land of love. *Aloha* more fully means "I see the divine in you and I see the divine in myself." Aloha expresses only one primary commandment:

Never to harm ...
... always to help.

In the Hawaiian teachings they believe if someone in the family has a problem then everyone has a problem. The same is of course true on larger scales of populations at national and global levels. We are becoming one global community in that what happens in one part of the world impacts all other parts of the world. We can no longer think sustainably in terms of us and them. We are all integral parts of this universe. As we're exploring in this self-discovery discussion, each of us is responsible for running our individual lives with integrity and compassion, so that we help engender a world community that's healthy, harmonious, sustainable and – let's say it right out loud – a pleasure to be a living participant in a greater whole.

Dr. Hew Len of Hawaii State University has developed an internal self-healing Ho'oponopono method for asking to be forgiven. None of us is perfect, we all make mistakes and do things that are unkind or even downright hurtful. Sometimes it's best to go face to face to the person we seek forgiveness from. At other times this isn't possible or advisable – but we can still go through the inner process of asking to be forgiven.

This process is all about cleansing oneself of pent-up negative emotions such as guilt, self-blame, shame and related feelings about a past deed we feel bad about and want to discharge from our system. And in the process, the outside world also gets cleaned – because each of us is intimately engaged with and ultimately one with the world. When even one heart is released from feeling guilt for a past action, the world is one step brighter.

I'd like to share with you this primary way to use the power and liberation of forgiveness for deepening your inner healing, and advancing your ongoing self-discovery adventure. When I pause to practice this daily meditation, I first get comfortable and tune into my breathing for a few deep breaths, to get centered. Then I bring to mind an image of the person I want to ask forgiveness for something I did to them or failed to do for them. Or something they did to me or failed to do for me.

I focus in my heart so that I can directly feel my heart's desire to ask to be forgiven, or to forgive them. I breathe into this desire, feel my love for this person, and my readiness to ask for forgiveness. Then I say to myself or in a whisper the first statement listed below. I say it several times until it's resonating deeply within me as a feeling, not just a thought.

Then I say the next statement in the same way, several times to myself. Then the third statement, and then the fourth. They're very short and simple statements – and yet they pack a beautiful power to evoke deep healing and transformation. And each time you move through this process with a different person, you'll go deeper into the experience. You might also want to do this process a number of times with the same person, in order to complete the inner reconciliation process:

I Love You ...

Please Forgive Me ...

I'm Sorry ...

Thank You

With the first statement, "I love you," make sure you actually feel this love in your heart before moving on to the next step. It is through bringing the power of love into this experience that you empower the process.

As you then say "Please forgive me," take time if you need to, and remember or relive the encounter or situation or outcome that you still feel bad about and want to resolve and move beyond. If it's a specific incident, you might say "Please forgive me ..." for whatever happened that you feel bad about. Note that you're not needing their forgiveness here, you're just clearing your own side of the equation.

And then with "I'm sorry," feel this in your heart also – open up to your sense of regret for what happened or didn't happen, but without blaming yourself, or the other person. You're just sorry that the person, or you yourself was hurt or damaged or left lacking or suffering.

The final statement is also key, because you're now actively closing the whole issue. Whether they're actually thanking you, you're thanking the universe for releasing you from this conflict. You're speaking high heart to high heart at spiritual levels, and concluding the process – feel thankful that you've removed the lingering weight on your heart. And if you don't feel closure, move through this same process over and over each day until you can fully let go and move on.

If you have the opportunity, do meet face to face and ask for forgiveness. But often this isn't possible. For instance many times someone (a parent for example) will die before there's resolution in your heart over something. No problem – you can do this if someone is gone from the earthly plane and it works equally well.

Also – it's not necessary to logically understand what you are doing in this process. The statements work like a sort of mantra, like a meditation. Just trust in the process and it will serve you well. It might not lead to the outcome you desire, but your highest good is always served – in this primal 4-step process you're turning it all over to your Higher Self, which remains mysterious to the ego mind.

As we've been exploring, part of you exists always in a higher spiritual state. Higher Consciousness is a knowing and wisdom far beyond words or explanations. Our challenge is to regularly pause and tap into our own inner guide, and open up to allow healing and insight to flow into our conscious minds. The more we do this, the more our ego learns to maintain its natural balance with our higher consciousness. And thus we continue apace on our inner discovery process.

CONCLUSION

We cannot force forgiveness – but we can readily explore its possibilities and its capacity to heal ourselves and sometimes even the person we're forgiving. Forgiveness helps us finish unfinished business. Forgiveness is an act of self-compassion. To me, forgiveness is a process that sets me free from the past. So many of us remain stuck in the grief of long-gone trauma, and thus are unable to experience our present lives fully.

Active forgiveness can change all this. We cannot choose to have a life free of hurt or pain, but we can choose to forgive and ask for forgiveness – and in the process liberate ourselves.

Self Discovery
Exercises And Meditations

~~~~~~~~~~~~~~~~~~~~~~

This book is a journey through your life which takes you to your past, encourages you to create your future, and then brings you back to the present. Here is a quick reference-guide and overview of the various exercises and meditations from each chapter. When you begin to use these exercises you will get results that assist you in becoming the successful and truly creative person you know you are meant to be.

Reflections On Chapter One
Beyond The Neurotic Ego

~~~~~~~~~~~~~~~~

Notice each morning when you wake up, how your ego mind instantly fixates on half a dozen lurking scenarios you need to deal with that day. Rather than enjoying the present moment and focusing on thankfulness just for being alive, you probably tend to run through your entire day in future-fixated worry/stress mode (anxiety) or past-fixated self-judgment and guilt/shame mode (depression). What we're focusing on in this book is your inner freedom and power to determine where you focus your attention moment to moment. You do have the power to choose – once you realize it.

~~~~~~~~~~~~~~~~

When you take your next shower, first of all notice if there's currently a negative flow of dialog that goes on in your mind between you and your inner critic. And then notice what happens when you choose to focus purely upon the present moment, on feeling good in your body, on breathing into
~~~~~~~~~~~~~~~~

newness – and see if without any provocation or pushing, you tap into something beyond your ego ... but something definitely you.

Reflections On Chapter Two

How We Save The World

~~~~~~~~~~~~~~~~

Whenever you catch yourself repeating nagging negative thoughts, shake them off at once. Refuse to be dragged down. And most important, choose wisely where to aim your attention in the next moment. When you wake up to the supposed battle in your ego-head, then the war in your head is over. And when you win the war in your head, you change your world. Sometimes when I'm in the shower and all this ego rubbish is running through my mind, I just shout out loud CANCEL, DELETE, SHUT UP. I tell it I am in charge and I choose right now to focus elsewhere.

~~~~~~~~~~~~~~~~

Next time you get triggered by what somebody calls you or does to you – ask yourself this question. What am I defending? You'll usually find that it's the ego's false image that you are defending. In reality the truth needs no defense – but the ego holds a false image of itself and therefore must fight back. We all have our imperfections and if we accept them, then the ego's false front becomes unnecessary.

~~~~~~~~~~~~~~~~

Every time you identify a negative quality in someone that you don't particularly like, pause for just a moment and see if you contain in some way that same negative quality within you that you're judging in the other person. If you can't see it within yourself, it's probably because you have repressed that
~~~~~~~~~~~~~~~~

quality. Your ego refuses to accept that it's not perfect. That can be a positive or negative quality.

~~~~~~~~~~~~~~~~

Here's a challenge I give to you: Get set up and take ten to fifteen minutes to sit and record yourself – give yourself permission to say whatever comes to mind, with zero censorship or self-editing of what is flowing spontaneously into your mind. Just let it all come spewing out with zero ego constraint. Instead, let your ego show itself! I guarantee you'll be amazed at the amount of rubbish that comes spewing forth, the same type of rubbish that fills your head and keeps you occupied 24/7.

~~~~~~~~~~~~~~~~

Also I challenge you to sit down and just write spontaneously for half an hour about whatever springs to mind, even if it's gibberish. You will perhaps be shocked to discover that you seem to have some nutter in there running the show.

~~~~~~~~~~~~~~~~

In *The Artist's Way* Julia Cameron talks about doing a morning writing meditation on a daily basis. I do this also, a brain dump that gets out into the open all the garbage and wisdom that's in your mind. By writing it down, somehow you get rid of the psychological luggage you woke up with. And after you write down what's lurking in your subconscious basement that morning, you don't need to read over it and evaluate it – just toss it away, and begin your day with a fresh open mind.

~~~~~~~~~~~~~~~~

You can take the exercise of writing down the garbage that is filling your mind, and apply it to receiving valued insights. This is an entire process in and of itself for tapping creative inflows. When you learn to feel quiet and peaceful and receptive inside, you can sit and breathe and allow Spirit by whatever name to gently and often deeply speak to you through spontaneous writing.

~~~~~~~~~~~~~~~

You may feel confused at times as to whether such inspiration is coming from the ego or the still small voice deeper within, but don't worry. If you stay tuned into your heart, you'll soon learn to discern your ego voice from your true voice. This is an ability I always help my clients develop. It's mostly a feeling in the heart. If it's your inner guide then something bubbles up brightly within you. And it's not an effort – it's just the opposite. It's a gift, a discovery, a helping hand.

Reflections On Chapter Three

Exploring Your Childhood

~~~~~~~~~~~~~~~

Are you still blindly following the basic way your parents did things?

Have you advanced to where you can question their beliefs, their habits, their attitudes?

What were the unspoken rules or injunctions passed on to you from your mother and father?

What was the quality, honesty, mutual respect and emotional depth of your parents' relationship?

How did they express love and handle all their various conflicts and emotions?

What was their style of parenting – were they authoritarian or permissive?

How did they handle conflict?

How did they handle money?

How where things resolved if there were disagreements?

Did they respect and value each other, or did they take each other for granted?

~~~~~~~~~~~~~~~~

I tell clients to pause and check in when they feel triggered by their partner, and ask a few simple questions of themselves:

What's the real source of this emotion?

Am I feeling like I did as a child?

What memory underlies this current unwanted feeling?

Reflections On Chapter Four

Our Inner Guidance System

~~~~~~~~~~~~~~~~

You might want to keep a note pad for a couple of weeks, and in each situation you move into, write down the dominant emotion you feel. This can be enlightening. Start to really get to know your dominant emotional style. And also notice if certain situations evoke certain emotions. When things go wrong or you're under stress, is it anxiety, anger, frustration, resentment, hopelessness or some other emotion that kicks into gear inside you in that situation? Feel, pay attention, reflect – and set yourself free.

~~~~~~~~~~~~~~~~

Begin to notice your underlying emotional personality traits. Who are you really in this regard? Do you see yourself as depressed, as an anxious person, as confused or aggressive emotionally? Don't try to analyze yourself – just be aware in an accepting mode. Seek to see the truth of you as an emotional being. Do you always see the world through the lens of one or two dominant emotions? Your emotional style or
~~~~~~~~~~~~~~~~

fixation might habitually be subjugation, failure, unlovability, perfectionism, vulnerability, anxiety.

Just keep watching – learn to accept who you really are! And in that process, you'll discover that you begin to change for the better. This is what self-discovery is all about ... being mindful of every moment inside your own body.

~~~~~~~~~~~~~~~~

For many people it may be difficult to allow or tolerate or even admit to certain feelings. We're often afraid that our feelings will overwhelm or even obliterate us if we open up to them. But I say to my clients, go ahead, let your heart break into a million pieces if it wants or needs to. Allow yourself to cry, to scream, to feel vulnerable if vulnerability arises in you. Learn to move toward your feelings rather than moving away from them. This is often challenging, but the results that emerge are well worth it.

Here's a key fact: feelings that arise have a natural life span. They can only remain with intensity for a short period of time. Can you feel surprised for an hour? Can you cry in despair for twenty minutes, or laugh with joy for ten? Start watching how your emotions come ... and go. This in itself can be liberating – almost always, even the most intense bad feelings will on their own come and go.

~~~~~~~~~~~~~~~~

A good question to ask when an intense feeling comes up is: "When in the past have I felt exactly this same way?" This question can be highly insightful, leading you to discover the origins of the feeling. When an intense emotion comes up and grabs at you, it's usually not just in reaction to your current situation. One of your emotional buttons is getting pushed. See if you can pause right in the middle of the reaction – and look to see what memories might spring to mind. Try to recall other times when you have had the same feeling. Go right into the heart of the feeling, and discover what is at the core.

Usually you'll find that there's some particular person in your past associated with the emotion you're feeling in the present. As we discussed earlier, we often attract people into our lives who enable us to feel whatever we've repressed, so that we can bring the original traumatic experience up in our memory, feel the original reaction we had, and open to healing and letting go of the memory. To feel it is to heal it – and we continue to be run by whatever we don't heal. Life is actually giving you a hand by presenting you with people who evoke unpleasant feelings buried within. Your challenge is to bring those early emotions up into conscious awareness.

Reflections On Chapter Five

Your Feelings Won't Kill You

~~~~~~~~~~~~~~~~

Listening to the message of the gut, and integrating this message into heart-felt impulses and higher reasoning – this is the path I find most effective in developing a better life.

And how is this done? Again – by focusing your power of attention directly toward your heart, and your gut – and developing that inner attention muscle so that you regularly look to your heart and gut to see what's going on there, before making decisions and going into action.

~~~~~~~~~~~~~~~~

Try this right now. Just become aware of your head, and all the 'thinking buzz' going on as you read these pages. And now shift your focus of awareness to your breathing ... and whatever feelings you might find in your heart right now. And ... just breathe into whatever feelings you discover. Allow that sensory information to become conscious in your thinking mind. Don't judge what you discover – just be aware, accept, and observe how this 'lower information' affects your higher mental processes.

You'll need to move through this process many times before it becomes a new valued habit. At first you'll want to take time – but after a while, wherever you are, you can instantly 'look down' and bring your deeper feelings to mind. Tune into the signals. Trust them. You've been conditioned not to trust your heart or your gut. I'm saying get beyond this conditioning. It takes time to educate your heart and gut to the fact that you now want to trust them, to listen to them. They have been out of the spotlight for so long, it might take them a while to find their own wisdom center. Just persevere. Become whole again!

~~~~~~~~~~~~~~~~

A good question to ask when an intense feeling comes up is: "When in the past have I felt exactly this same way?" This question can be highly insightful, leading you to discover the origins of the feeling. When an intense emotion comes up and grabs at you, it's usually not just in reaction to your current situation. One of your emotional buttons is getting pushed. See if you can pause right in the middle of the reaction – and look to see what memories might spring to mind. Try to recall other times when you have had the same feeling. Go right into the heart of the feeling, and discover what is at the core.

Usually you'll find that there's some particular person in your past associated with the emotion you're feeling in the present.

When someone triggers you, if you are honest and in touch with yourself you can own the upset and throw no blame. You can say "Aha – this is a great opportunity to see something inside of myself that needs to be witnessed, accepted, looked
~~~~~~~~~~~~~~~~

at and released." People might trigger my fear, for instance – but not cause it. Understanding this dynamic can eliminate loads of present-moment conflict.

Reflections On Chapter Six

Are You Waiting To Be Happy?

~~~~~~~~~~~~~~~~

I challenge you to put down this book right now and answer honestly this question: *WHAT AM I WAITING FOR?*

The message here is very clear – stop waiting and start living.

~~~~~~~~~~~~~~~~

Ask the question of yourself: are you just trudging along mindlessly toward your retirement, feeling mostly unhappy while waiting to be happy then? The solution is clear: choose to be happy now, regardless of your life situation.

~~~~~~~~~~~~~~~~

Just pause for a few breaths, get grounded in your breathing and your whole body – and ask yourself the following question: "Am I living right now ... or am I wishing my life away, waiting for the good times to come?"

You have really only one moment in your hands – this moment right now. Either you open up and fully experience it or you leave it unlived, waiting on the promise of tomorrow.
~~~~~~~~~~~~~~~~

Reflections On Chapter Seven

Worry Is A Wasted Emotion

~~~~~~~~~~~~~~~~

Worrying will add nothing to your life. So don't waste your time and energy in futile worrying. There are a number of successful programs that life coaches guide their clients through, and many books that are helpful as well, and online programs also. But it's your choice to act in this direction. If you're a worrier and suffering as a result – act! And the first act is to begin watching your own mind in action. Watch a worried thought pop into your mind. Look to see where it came from – your own possible future demise – about dying.

~~~~~~~~~~~~~~~~

So hey, begin to look honestly at who you really are, and how you're at some point going to cease to exist. Get used to the idea. Learn to accept reality at this level – it's the shortest route to less worry and more enjoyment of the time you have left on Earth.

~~~~~~~~~~~~~~~~

Remember you are a creative being, and your thoughts are the creative agent busy manifesting your visions, dreams, worries and so forth. I sometimes feel that worrying about something is actually like putting in a request to the universe and asking for it to happen. There is no worry in nature, as we discussed before. Humans are the thinkers – and we reap what we sow.

~~~~~~~~~~~~~~~~

If you are worried that there is a boogie man in your wardrobe, shine a light in the wardrobe and see the truth. That's the end of the worrying. Deal with the worry – and be done with it.

Reflections On Chapter Eight

Your Yin/Yang Balance

~~~~~~~~~~~~~~~~

So the question is: When you look deeply to your own inner condition, what do you feel you need more or less of? Not 'what do you *want* more of' but 'what do you *need* more of,' in order to be balanced within your true nature? In what realms of your being do you perhaps need to focus loving attention and alter your male-female stance in life?

~~~~~~~~~~~~~~~~

And while dealing with this dualistic yin/yang balance, let's always continue to remember the yin-yang unity symbol, where optimally there's a higher sense of unity and oneness surrounding the merger of yin and yang. When we're overly fixated on yang energy we over-value productivity and action, and consider inaction to be a sign of weakness. When we're obsessed with speed and data, when we're caught up in a whirlwind of yang madness and endless busyness, we also are prone to chronic anxiety and stress-related illnesses.

~~~~~~~~~~~~~~~~

Here's a clue to finding inner balance. Feminine energy is *experientially focused*, whereas masculine energy is *results-oriented.* We need both of these energies to survive and thrive. And while yin and yang are opposite of one another, this doesn't mean they are oppositional or in conflict. Instead they complement each other.

~~~~~~~~~~~~~~~~

Take some time to contemplate these elicitor questions:

> *Do you often experience an inability to ease up, relax and let go?*
>
> *Are you habitually a judgmental person?*

Have you a need for constant stimulation, and maybe can't sit still and just be content with yourself?

Do you want to create space in your life for pausing and reflecting before leaping into action?

Do you find yourself feeling low on energy to where you just sit around and don't accomplish anything?

Do you let people love you just as you are?

And who do you accept and love unconditionally?

~~~~~~~~~~~~~~~~

We do need to recognize when to act and when to step back, when to pursue relentlessly and when to wait patiently – when to offer to bring the impetus of profound harmony to our daily lives and when to allow things to resolve themselves without interruption. And if we hold the goal of balance always in our minds, even when we temporarily go to extremes we can still swiftly regain equilibrium.

Reflections On Chapter Nine

Discover Your Vision

~~~~~~~~~~~~~~~~

Please pause and answer this question:

What is your primary goal
at this moment in your life?

If you can't answer that question right away then you are probably not clear regarding your higher passion in life. You might very well be just drifting along in existing family and work ruts, allowing the events and circumstances around you to be the driving force in your life. You might see yourself as 'poor me' and an innocent victim – but nothing could be further from the truth. As we've been seeing in this book, no one but you is determining the myriad of choices that you make day in and day out. If you make just a slight change in your routine or attitude, and then make another, and another, your life does change!

~~~~~~~~~~~~~~~~

Ask these questions of yourself:

What was I brought into existence to accomplish?

What situations most energize me?

What am I most passionate about?

In what ways do I see myself as a hero?

Deep inside my hopeful heart, what springs to mind as a new vision for my optimum future?

~~~~~~~~~~~~~~~~

But here's the reality-orient: simply wishing for success to come into your life isn't enough. You need to nurture a vision and then each day act on it! Your vision will provide you with a sense of direction and enduring hope – an authentic reason for living. If you feel content, great. But if not, don't spend your life slaving away doing work you don't like with people you don't resonate with.

~~~~~~~~~~~~~~~~

If you want to be acknowledged, acknowledge yourself.

If you want to be valued, value yourself.

If you want to be accepted, accept yourself.

If you want to be seen, see yourself.

If you want to be heard, listen to yourself.
~~~~~~~~~~~~~~~~

If you want to feel loved – love yourself!

Whatever you want from other people, you can learn to give it to yourself. Be your own advocate in your own life. Learn to nurture a mind of your own.

~~~~~~~~~~~~~~~~

I recommend making your vision far-reaching, requiring a stretch to accomplish. Your vision is best seen as an on-going dream that you are striving to move fully into.

Nurture your vision, choose a long-term focus and commitment, have an ever-evolution plan of action – and stay the course until you begin to get results. A vision without a plan is a fantasy. A vision with a plan is a happening.

~~~~~~~~~~~~~~~~

Gently over time, develop your vision of the day-to-day life you want to manifest, the things you truly want, the household ambiance that will nurture your inner growth, the job that resonates with your personal intentions, the relationships that sustain you emotionally, the quality of each new day you would like to enjoy – what in fact is your ideal day, week, month, year? Do you want to spend the rest of your life dreading that Monday feeling, or do you want to create the life you spirit and soul really years for?

~~~~~~~~~~~~~~~~

Answer this question spontaneously:

What is your number one core value for your life?

If you can't answer this question, perhaps you have never given much thought to what your core values and primary virtues are. With clients I often have them reflect on and identify their top five core values. Then in the spirit of self-discovery I have them look deeply to see if their lives are
~~~~~~~~~~~~~~~~

aligned and congruent with their core values. You might want to do this yourself as a basic insight adventure.

~~~~~~~~~~~~~~~~

What must you have in life to experience fulfillment?

What values are ESSENTIAL to your life?

What virtues represent your PRIMARY WAY OF BEING?

Reflections On Chapter Ten

The Fine Art Of Forgiveness

~~~~~~~~~~~~~~~~

What about you – how do you stand in regard to each of these dis-ease causing emotions? Take a deep breath and see how you respond to these questions:

Am I still hanging on to an old hurt?

Is my heart feeling hardened to someone?

Am I often caught up in angry feelings?

Is there someone I really need to forgive?

Can I forgive myself?

~~~~~~~~~~~~~~~~

Sometimes I get my clients who are working toward forgiveness to write a letter that they won't send to the person they are trying to forgive. Writing an uncensored letter is a great way to let it all pour out onto the pages – just consciously acknowledge all the inner feelings that come up as a result of writing the letter. As you bring your pent-up emotions out into the open through the letter, a definite healing takes place through that 'revealing' process. In fact whenever you feel buried emotions under pressure inside you, polluting your
~~~~~~~~~~~~~~~~

thoughts and actions, this method of writing down what you're feeling is an excellent thing to do.

~~~~~~~~~~~~~~~~

And whenever your life feels stuck, pause, tune into your breathing and your heart – and ask yourself without forethought the question: *Who is it that I need to forgive?*

~~~~~~~~~~~~~~~~

Here's a primary way to use the power and liberation of forgiveness for deepening your inner healing, and advancing your ongoing self-discovery adventure. First get comfortable and tune into your breathing for a few deep breaths, to get centered.

Now bring to mind an image of the person you want to ask to be forgiven for something you did to them or failed to do for them. – or something they did to you or failed to do for you.

Focus in your heart so that you can directly feel your heart's desire to ask to be forgiven, or to forgive them. Breathe into this desire, feel your love for this person, and your readiness to ask for forgiveness. Then say silently to yourself or in a whisper the first statement listed below. Say it several times until it's resonating deeply within you as a feeling, not just a thought.

Now say the next statement in the same way several times. And then the third statement, and then the fourth. They're very short and simple statements – and yet they pack a beautiful power to evoke deep healing and transformation.

Each time you move through this process with a different person, you'll go deeper into the experience. You might also want to do this process a number of times with the same person, in order to complete the inner reconciliation process:

I Love You ...

Please Forgive Me ...

I'm Sorry ...

Thank You

With the first statement, "I love you," make sure you actually feel this love in your heart before moving on to the next step. It is through bringing the power of love into this experience that you empower the process.

As you then say "Please forgive me," take time if you need to, and remember or relive the encounter or situation or outcome that you still feel bad about and want to resolve and move beyond. If it's a specific incident, you might say "Please forgive me ..." for whatever happened that you feel bad about. Note that you're not needing their forgiveness here, you're just clearing your own side of the equation.

And then with "I'm sorry," feel this in your heart also – open up to your sense of regret for what happened or didn't happen, but without blaming yourself, or the other person. You're just sorry that the person, or you yourself was hurt or damaged or left lacking or suffering.

The final statement is also key, because you're now actively closing the whole issue. Whether they're actually thanking you, you're thanking the universe for releasing you from this conflict. You're speaking high heart to high heart at spiritual levels, and concluding the process – feel thankful that you've removed the lingering weight on your heart. And if you don't feel closure, move through this same process over and over each day until you can fully let go and move on.

~~~~~~~~~~~~~~~~
~~~~~~~~~~~~~~~~

ACKNOWLEDGMENTS

~~~~~~~~~~~~~~~~~~~~~~~~~~~~

In the Month of May, 2023 while I was writing this book, my younger brother Frederick got a terminal diagnosis of cancer and was told he had six to nine months to live. He was living in West Cork. So my trips up and down to West Cork during the summer to visit Fred really brought the topics in this book into sharp focus. Each time I left West Cork and drove back to Dublin, I never knew if it was the last time I would see Fred.

So cherishing every moment and having true connection with him became so important to me. I saw first-hand how all of Fred's current *fears and worries* just vanished into thin air. I myself decided to let go of *waiting* for my book to be perfect, before I let someone read it. Fred was the first person to read the first draft of my book, his encouragement and feedback were very affirming.

Fred passed away on the fourth of November, 2023. This book is dedicated to him.

Thanks to my sister-in-law Eileen Murphy and her husband Pat for lending me their house in the countryside of Waterford, while they were on vacation, so I could concentrate on my writing with no distractions and in beautiful surroundings. Thanks to my niece, Aisling Conneely from Spiddal, Co. Galway for her artistic creativity in designing the cover for my book.

Thanks to Denise Moroney and Fran McDonnell for the powerful, experiential seminars and trainings they teach on the principals of *A Course in Miracles*, in Tralee, Co. Kerry. I
~~~~~~~~~~~~~~~~~~~~~~~~~~~~

have learnt so much from these trainings over the past 15 years. Denise and Fran are the living embodiment of the yin/yang energy in action.

Thanks to my Life Coach Henk Schram from Holland, for coaching me for the last year and a half, and keeping me focused and holding me accountable to realize my vision of writing and publishing my book.

Last but definitely not least, I would like to give a heartfelt thanks and sincere gratitude from the bottom of my heart to John Selby for his amazing contribution, wisdom and creativity. John definitely has the gift of discernment and has such a keen sense of perception. His professional guidance and how he put structure and flow into this book have been invaluable.

I love the synchronicity of how John and I connected. I first made a firm and irrevocable decision to finish and publish my book in 2023. I put that call out into the universe ... and John answered that call, and immediately resonated with the message in this book. I am deeply thankful to John for getting my book to the finish line.

NAMASTE

Linda Parsons – Bio

~~~~~~~~~~~~~~~~~~~~~~~~~~~~

Linda Reilly Parsons was born in Drogheda, Co. Louth.

After her leaving Cert she went to college to study Business Studies and then worked in the area of finance for a couple of years. She then decided to study psychology which was always a keen interest of hers. She did various trainings in psychotherapy, yoga teaching and dietetics. In 1995 she moved to Malahide, Co. Dublin where she met her husband Colm. They were together for 15 years. Colm developed a condition called trigeminal neuralgia. Soon after his diagnosis Colm spiraled into a dark depression and sadly couldn't live with this pain any longer. Colm died by suicide in 2010. During this grieving period in her life, Linda realized the high cost of dwelling on a sense of sadness and despair and fixating on the negative. Linda believes that if you realized how powerful your thoughts are, you would never think negatively for very long. Linda firmly believes that our minds are creative, whether in the positive or the negative, and that our most valuable asset in life is our minds. She believes that we are the masters of our fate, the captain of our souls.

Linda has been working with clients for over 30 years now. Linda worked in a Child and Family Centre working with families in a disadvantaged area in North Dublin. She also worked in the area of domestic violence for 10 years, supporting and empowering women with skills and strategies for dealing with abusive relationships. Linda designed a program called "*The Three Keys to Self-Empowerment*" which is a support-group program for victims and survivors of gender based domestic violence and abuse, and is based on three vital questions. Linda trained various facilitators all around Ireland so that they could run this group program in
~~~~~~~~~~~~~~~~~~~~~~~~~~~~

their area. Linda also implemented the NVR program (Non-Violent Resistance) for families affected by child-to-parent violence. Linda has done extensive studying and training on NPD (Narcissistic Personality Disorder) and the impact of different forms of psychological abuse.

In 2016 Linda did a two-year diploma course in Life and Workplace Coaching. She then started working as a Life Coach. She now implements her own innovative approach to coaching, which is a hybrid of psychotherapy and coaching. Her passion is to empower and inspire her clients to overcome life challenges and tap into their inner potential and creative spirit. Linda sees life as an ongoing adventure into ever-deeper self-discovery.

Following her husband's death, Linda got a beautiful dog named Ruby. She says her dog is not just a dog ... he keeps her sane, he makes her happy and he is her coach, the best listener ever. Linda thinks that the world would be a nicer place if everyone had the ability to love as unconditionally as her dog Ruby.

Resources, Contacts, etc.

~~~~~~~~~~~~~~~~~~~~~~~~~~~~~~~~~~~~~

Linda's Contact Info:

lindaparsonsselfdiscovery.com

lindaparsonselfdiscovery@gmail.com

~~~~~~~~~~~~~~~~~~~

Resource Books

Alice Miller, 1991, The Untouched Key, Random House, N.Y.

Alice Miller, 1985, Thou Shalt Not Be Aware, Pluto Press, 345 Archway Road, London N6 5AA

Bethany Webster, 2021, Discovering the Inner Mother, Harper Collins Publishers, 195 Broadway, New York, NY 10007.

Claude Steiner, 1990, Scripts People Live, Grove Atlantic, 841 Broadway, New York, NY 10003.

Don Miguel Ruiz, 1997, The Four Agreements, Amber-Allen Publishing Inc. P.O. Box 6657, San Rafael, California 94903.

Don Miguel Ruiz, Don Jose Ruiz, 2010, The Fifth Agreement, Amber-Allen Publishing Inc, P.O. Box 6657, San Rafael, California 94903.

Dr Arthur Janov, 1993, The New Primal Scream, Clays Ltd, St. Ives plc, Great Britain.

Eckhart Tolle, 2005, The Power of Now, Hodder and Stoughton Ltd, 338 Euston Road, London NW1 3BH.

John Lee, 2010, Growing Yourself Back Up, Three Rivers Press, New York.

Julia Cameron, 1995, The Artist's Way, Macmillan Publishers Ltd, 25 Eccleston Place, London, SW1W 9NF and Basing Stoke.

Louise Hay, 1991, The Power is Within You, Hay House UK Ltd, the sixth floor, Watson House, 54 Baker Street, London WIU 7BU.

Louise Hay, 1989, Heal Your Body, Eden Grove Editions, 8 The Arena, Mollison Avenue, Enfield, Middlesex EN3 7NJ.

Louise Hay, 2005, You Can Heal Your Life, Hay House UK Ltd, Watson House, 54 Baker Street, London WIU 7BU.

Robert Burney, 2011, Codependence The Dance of Wounded Souls, Joy to You & Me Enterprises, P.O. Box 235401, Emanitas, California 92023.

Ross Rosenberg, 2013, The Human Magnet Syndrome, PESI Publishing and Media, 3839 White Avenue, Eau Claire 54702.

Robert Fritz, 2003, Your life As Art, Newfane Press, P.O. Box 189, Newfane VT 05 345.

Robert Fritz, 1989, The Path of Least Resistance, Ballatine books, division of Random House, Inc, New York.

Stephen Levin, 1997, A Year to Live, Beacon Press, 25 Beacon Street, Boston MA 02108

Stephen Wolinsky, 1993, The Dark Side of The Inner Child, Bramble Books, United States of America.

Viktor Frankl, 1984, Man's Search for Meaning, Beacon Press, 25 Beacon Street, Boston MA 02108

~~~~~~~~~~~~~~~~~~~~~~~~~~~~~~~~
~~~~~~~~~~~~~~~~~~~~~~~~~~~~~~~~

www.ingramcontent.com/pod-product-compliance
Lightning Source LLC
LaVergne TN
LVHW020711110826
845149LV00012B/2218
* 9 7 8 1 9 6 2 9 8 4 1 6 4 *